CHAPTER 1

INTRODUCTION

Many of us enjoy photographing birds, whatever our level of expertise. Birds can be engaging and intriguing creatures and we in Australia have some of the most spectacular and fascinating birds in the world in our backyards and within easy reach of major population centres.

Each year (usually in October), the nation's premier independent bird conservation organisation BirdLife Australia conducts the Aussie Bird Count asking people to list the birds they've seen within a 20 minute period, either their own backyard, a local park or

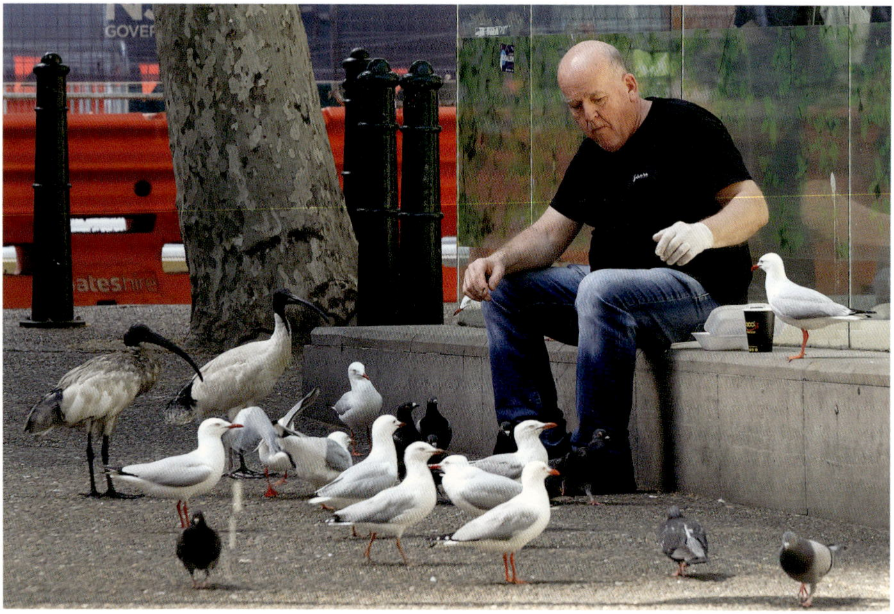

People have long been attracted to birds, even common species like Silver Gulls, Pigeons and White Ibis. Fujifilm X-T3 camera with XF 55-200mm f/3.5-4.9 R LM OIS lens at 200mm (300mm equivalent in 35mm format); ISO 800, 1/160 second at f/8; Aperture-priority AE with centre-weighted metering.

beach or even a town centre. They also run seasonal *Birds In Backyards* surveys four times a year and publish the results nationwide. (See Chapter 3.)

They also run a special website for photographers at www.birdlifephotography.org.au with links to articles, video tutorials, news on competitions and conferences as well as a gallery of members' images.

Ethical considerations

Around the world, birds are under threat from climate change and loss of habitat. Complicating matters is an increase in the number of bird photographers since the beginning of the 21st century, fuelled by more capable equipment and greater opportunities to travel to previously protected places.

These factors are having a cumulative impact and all photographers must take them into account. Some birds are particularly vulnerable, especially during their breeding seasons. Finding nesting sites and food for growing chicks can be highly competitive; predators abound and any injury or stress-induced illness can cause death, especially in young bird families.

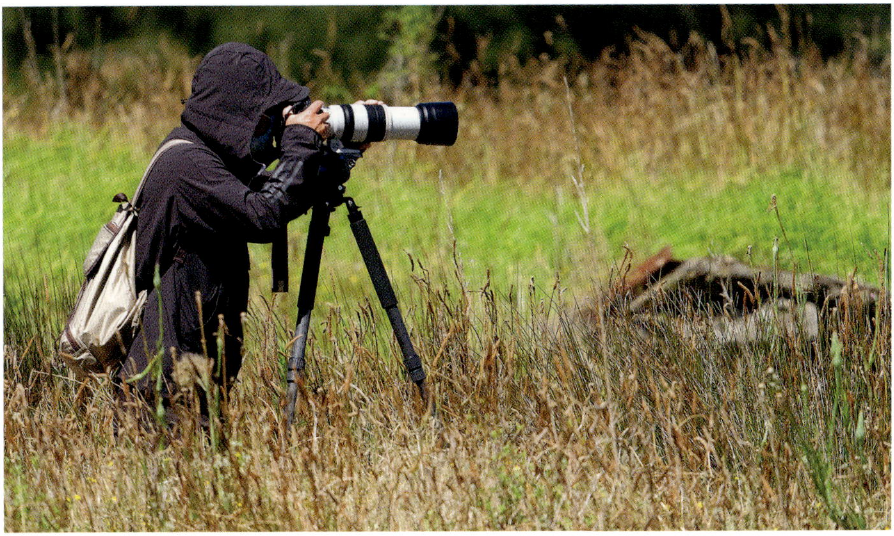

As more photographers seek out close-up shots of birds, pressure is mounting on bird habitats, particularly those close to urban areas. If these areas are not protected the birds will disappear. Fujifilm X-T3 camera with Tamron 150-500mm f/5-6.7 DiIII VC VXD lens at 500mm (750mm equivalent in 35mm format), ISO 320, 1/500 second at f/6.7.

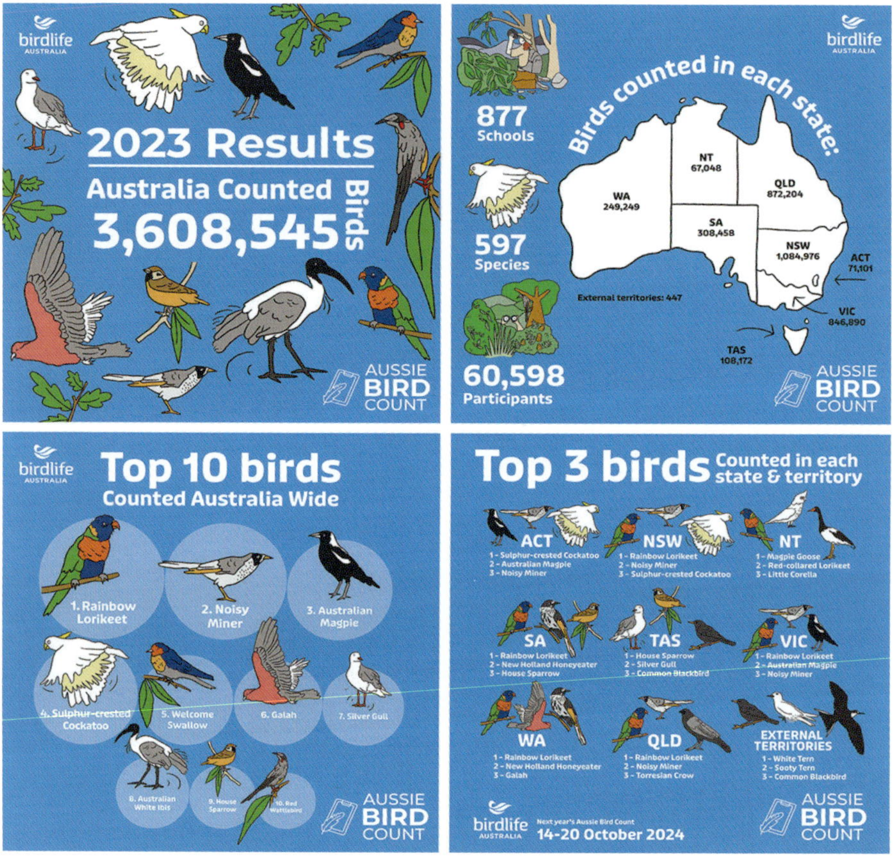

Four graphics showing the results of the 2023 Aussie Bird Count. (Source: BirdLife Australia.)

Predators are often attracted by the presence of people so you need to act accordingly. Check out BirdLife Australia's downloadable set of Ethical Birdwatching Guidelines at www.tinyurl.com/birdwatch-ethics for advice on safe behaviour – for you and the birds you want to photograph.

Be especially careful when birds are **nesting**. Don't disturb birds in, at or near nests. This is so important that photographs of nests with eggs or chicks in them are *not* accepted for publication on any BirdLife Photography site, regardless of whether a parent bird

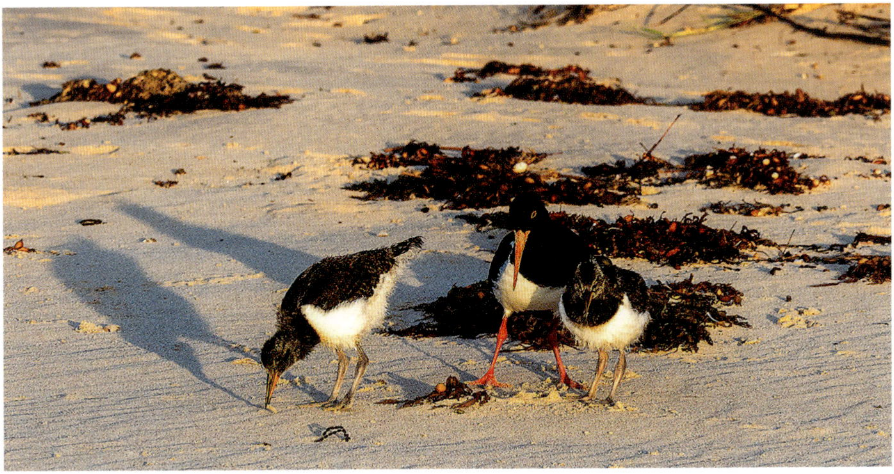

Beach-nesting birds like this Pied Oystercatcher are extremely vulnerable to disturbance. The beach where this mother and her half-grown chicks were photographed is well signposted and off-limits to dogs during the breeding season. OM-D E-M1 II camera with M. Zuiko Digital ED 12-100mm f4.0 IS PRO lens at 100mm (200mm in 35mm equivalent), ISO 200, 1/250 second at f/5.6.

is present and whether the birds seem comfortable having humans around.

Beach-nesting birds are particularly vulnerable to disturbance and predation so you should avoid visiting locations with nesting sites during the breeding season. All relevant regulations and local signs should be obeyed.

The same applies to the more than 70% of Australian bird species that use **hollows** for roosting, nesting or both. Some local councils and conservation bodies provide nesting boxes as substitutes where few natural hollows exist.

In general you should follow these guidelines:

- Don't touch nests or young birds. Call WIRES or another similar organisation or contact a local vet if you find a fledgling that has fallen out of a nest.
- Don't trample or otherwise damage vegetation around a bird's resting or nesting place.
- Don't startle birds. This can cause them to accidentally break or eject the eggs or nestlings from the nest.
- Stay clear of nesting areas during the breeding season in the early mornings,

around dusk or during inclement weather. If the parents desert the nest the eggs or young will become cold and die.

- Don't use a flash to photograph birds – especially when they are on or near a nest.

Many local authorities put up signs during the breeding season warning people in the area to keep away.

Magpies and other swoopers

Most Australians are well aware of the Magpie swooping season between August and October when the birds defend their nests. During this period, the Magpies attack anything they consider to be a threat – not just humans.

Magpies are remarkably clever. They can remember the faces of people in their areas who are non-threatening and won't attack these people. While they rarely swoop in Tasmania, those that swoop in other states only do so within about 100 metres of their nests, so they're easily avoided by staying clear of known nesting areas.

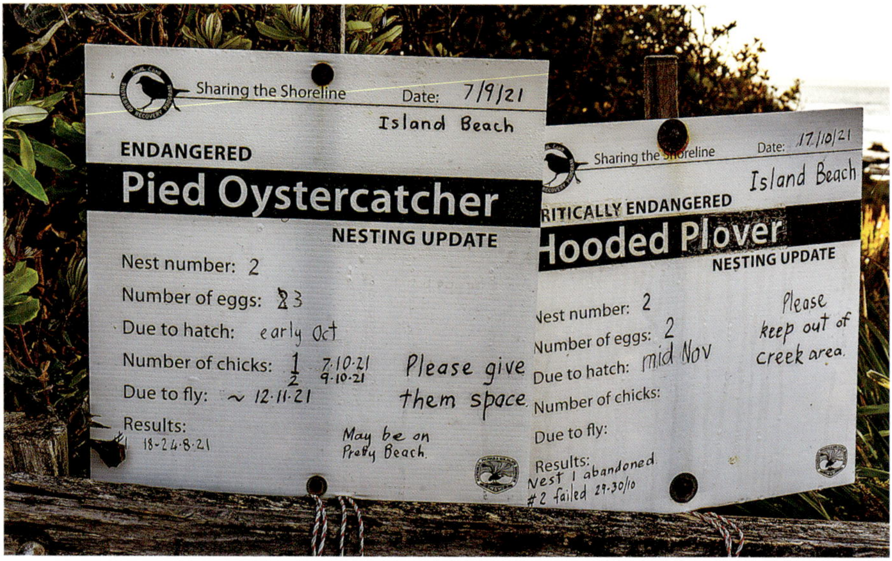

Signs posted at the entry point to the beach where the above photo was taken advising visitors about nesting birds.

If you can't avoid being in an area where the local Magpies don't know you during the breeding season, follow these guidelines:

1. Play it cool and keep low-key. If you act aggressively or shout, the Magpies will see you as a threat not just for the current year, but for up to five years to come.

2. Walk, don't run, and avoid making eye contact with the birds.

3. Wear sunglasses and a broad-brimmed hat – or carry an open umbrella above your head.

4. Travel in groups; swooping birds normally only target individuals.

5. Cyclists should walk their bikes through magpie territory or have a flag on the back of the bike that extends above their head.

6. Don't feed swooping Magpies as it can encourage swooping behaviour.

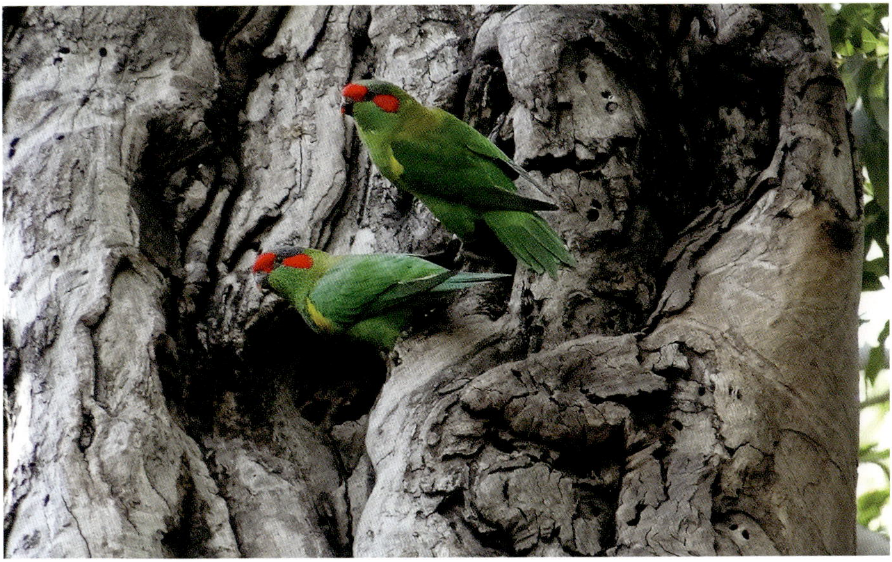

Many parrots, rosellas and lorikeets, like these Musk Lorikeets, nest in the hollows in old growth trees. Don't intrude on their nesting sites, particularly if there's a chance they may have eggs or chicks. Sony DSC-HX1 fixed-lens camera at 100mm focal length, ISO 1000, 1/160 second at f/5.2.

Masked Lapwings (often called plovers) are another bird that regularly swoops on intruders during the breeding season. Because they nest on the ground (often in grassy woodlands, paddocks and playing fields), their chicks are particularly vulnerable. Avoid intruding on their territories during the breeding season between July and November.

Kookaburras are known to swoop down and steal food from picnickers at almost any time of year. But they can also attack perceived threats (including their reflections in windows) during the breeding season from September to January.

Red Wattlebirds can also swoop and snap their beaks if a person passes close to their nests during the breeding season from July to December. Noisy Miners and wattlebirds will also swoop to defend their territory all year round.

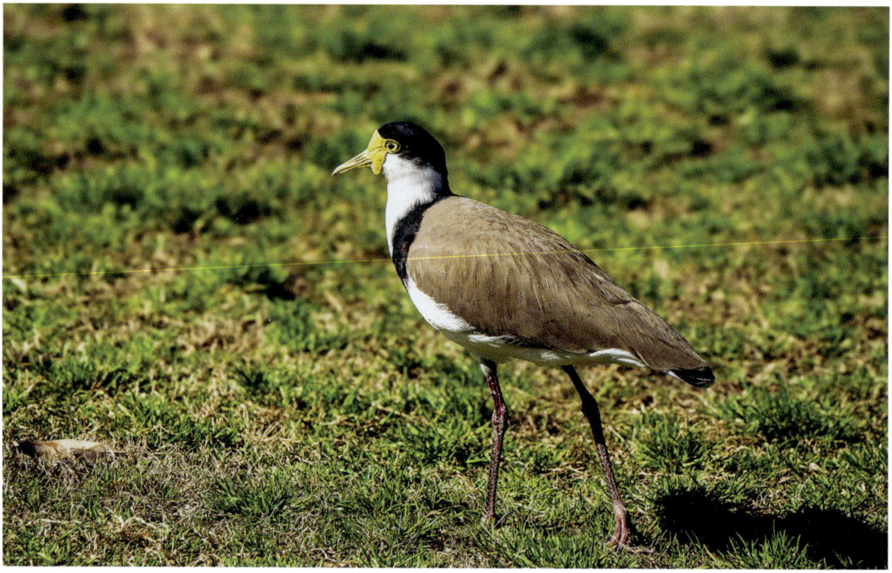

Masked Lapwings nest on the ground, often in parks, school ovals, golf courses, sports fields and open paddocks. They are common across northern, eastern and southern Australia but absent from Western Australia. They only swoop during a three-week period when they have eggs or small chicks to care for. Sony ILCE-7M3 camera with Tamron 50-400mm f/4.5-6.3 Di III VC VXD lens at 400mm, ISO 320, 1/500 second at f/11, Aperture-priority AE, centre-weighted metering.

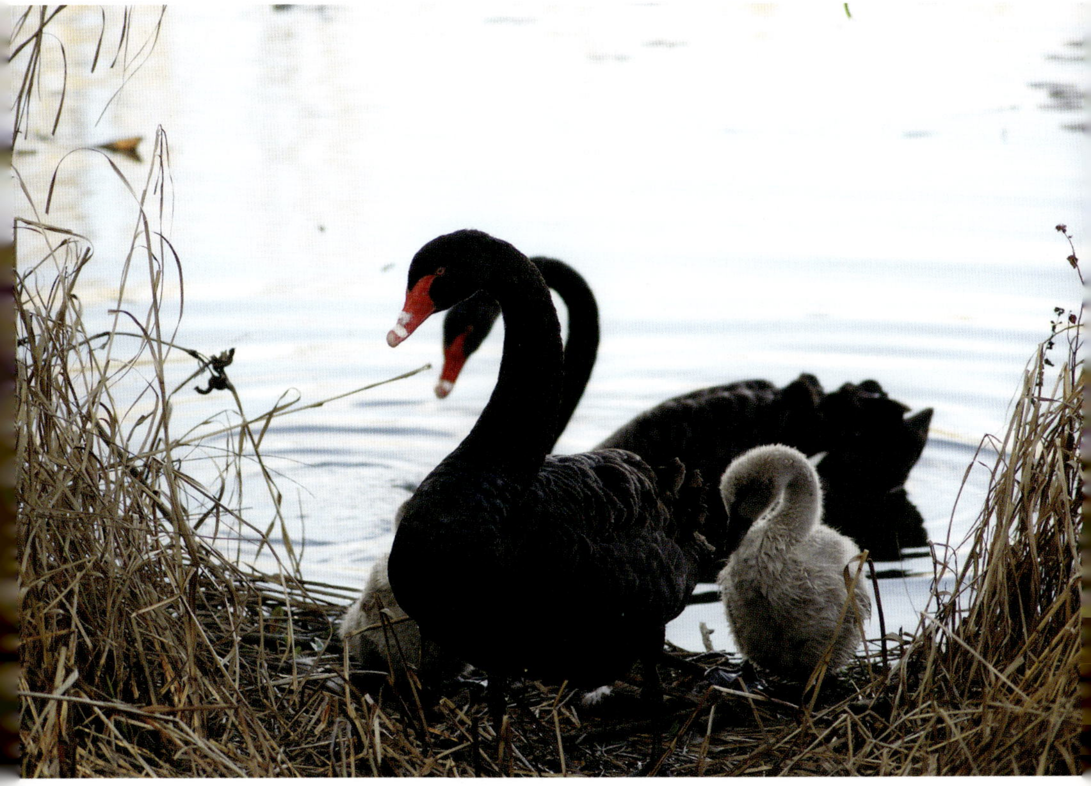

Keep well clear of birds when they have chicks – and don't use a flash when photographing them. Some birds, such as Swans, attack people who come too close to their chicks. Sony DSLR-A230 camera (vintage 2009) with DT 18-250mm f/3.5-6.3 lens at 135mm (202mm equivalent in 35mm format), ISO 100, 1/100 second at f/5, Aperture-priority AE, multi-pattern metering.

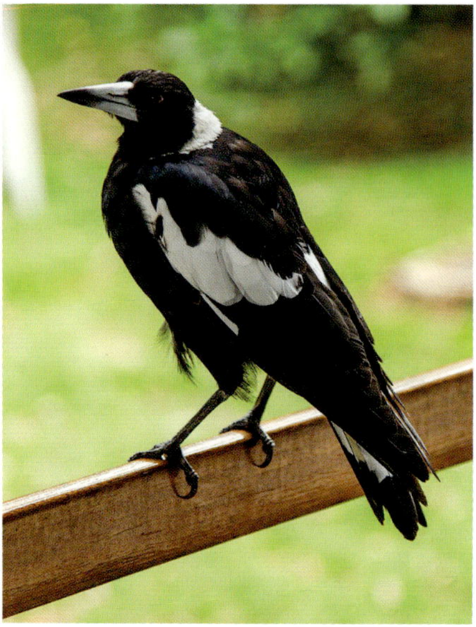

Magpies often swoop on strangers during their breeding season – although they seldom trouble people they are familiar with and rarely swoop beyond about 100 metres of their nests. Nikon D7000 camera with 24-120mm f/4 lens at 120mm (180mm in 35mm format), ISO 200, 1/30 second at f/4, Program AE with centre-weighted metering.

Powerful Owls defend their territory year-round and have been known to swoop during the breeding season between April and September. You won't hear them coming due to their silent flight. With expanding populations of their main prey (possums), in built-up areas these owls are increasingly being recorded in suburban areas east of the Great Dividing Range, from south-eastern Queensland to Victoria.

Getting started

Bird photography presents a number of challenges. Your subjects can be highly mobile, flighty and fast-moving and they're often found in out-of-the-way places. Decide which kinds of birds you want to photograph, where you're most likely to find them and the kind of equipment that will give you the best results.

Techniques and equipment will be different for photographing birds in flight and when taking close-ups from a hide. Chapter 6 in this guide outlines the best camera settings to use in different situations and for obtaining different kinds of shots.

It also covers autofocusing and drive modes, how to record backlit subjects and subjects in contrasty lighting, and how far you can push ISO settings when working in dim lighting and/or with slow telephoto lenses. We also provide some references to help you take your photography further.

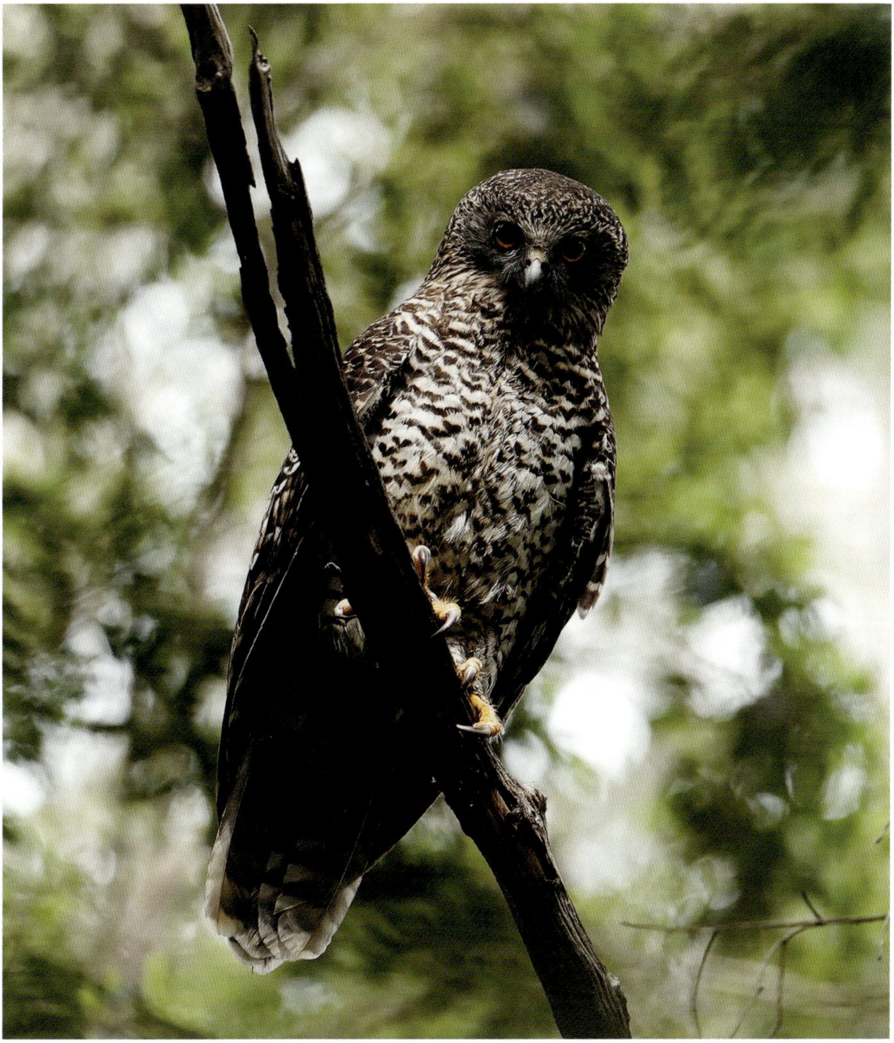

The largest of Australia's owls is the Powerful Owl, which lives in the moist forests of eastern Australia. Powerful Owls are known to defend their territory all year-round – and you won't hear one coming if you trespass on its territory. Sony ILCE-9 camera with FE 70-200mm f/2.8 GM OSS lens at 197mm, ISO 800, 1/1000 second at f/2.8, Aperture-priority AE, centre-weighted metering.

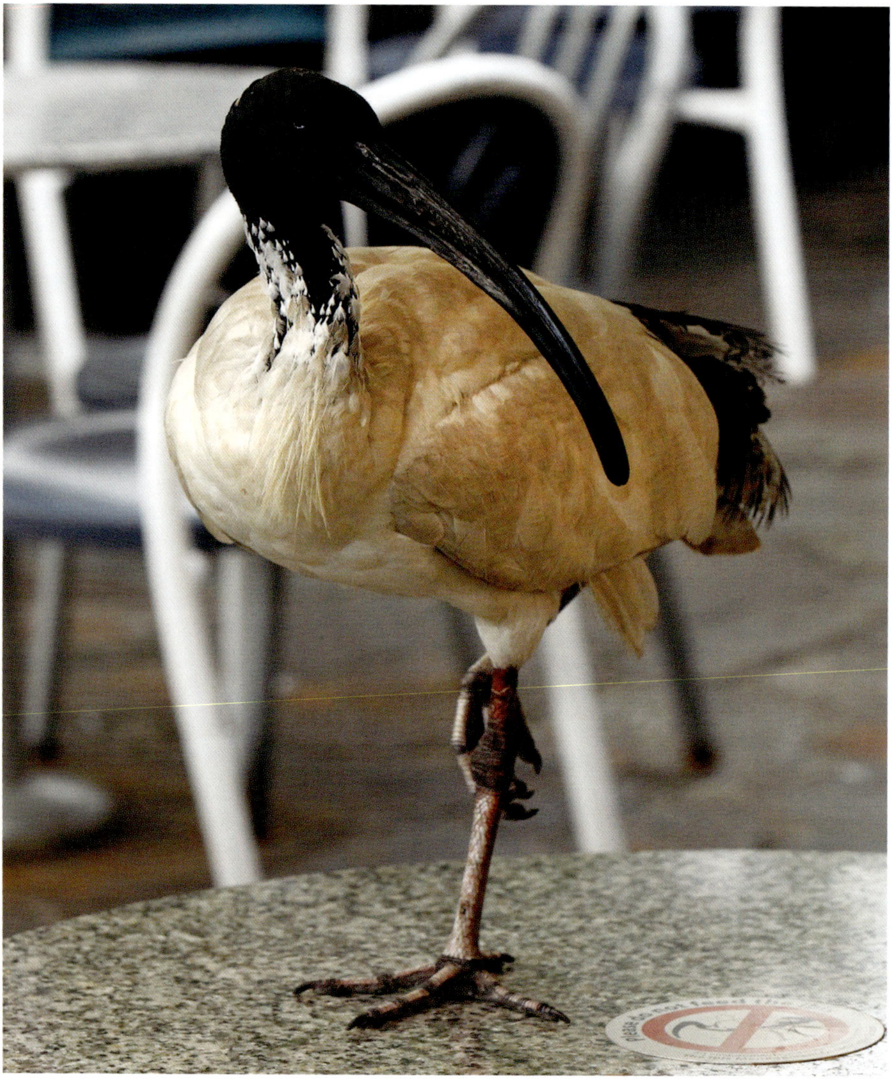

It's not difficult to find and photograph common urban birds like White Ibis when they come to you in search of food scraps. Canon EOS-1D Mark IV camera with EF 70-200mm f/2.8L IS III USM lens at 102mm, ISO 3200, 1/160 second at f/6.3, Aperture-priority AE, multi-pattern metering.

CHAPTER 2

EQUIPMENT

While any camera can be used to capture images of birds, some features can make it much easier. Fast, accurate autofocus tracking and snappy burst speeds can help you grab the shot, while a sharp lens and adequate resolution ensure it looks good. Many recent cameras include subject-detection autofocus, which can recognise subjects like birds. For 'bird in flight', or BIF photography, this can be a true game-changer.

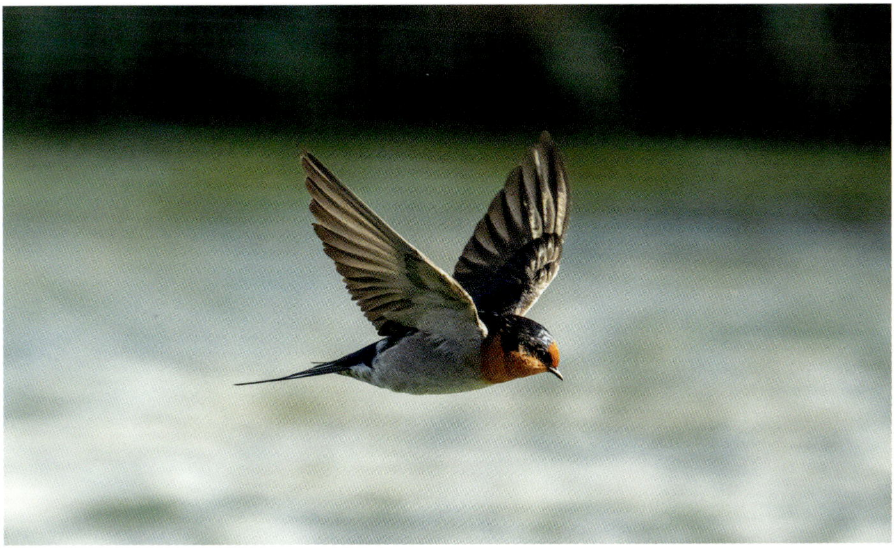

The latest high-end cameras, like the Nikon Z 8 used by Dani Webb of Camera House Croydon in Victoria to record this shot of a tiny Welcome Swallow in flight, provide subject-detection autofocusing and tracking to aid photographers in such situations. Being in the right place, setting the right exposure parameters and tracking the subject are also keys to success. Nikkor Z 180-600mm f/5.6-6.3 VR lens at 600mm, ISO 800, 1/2500 second at f/6.3, spot metering. © Dani Webb.

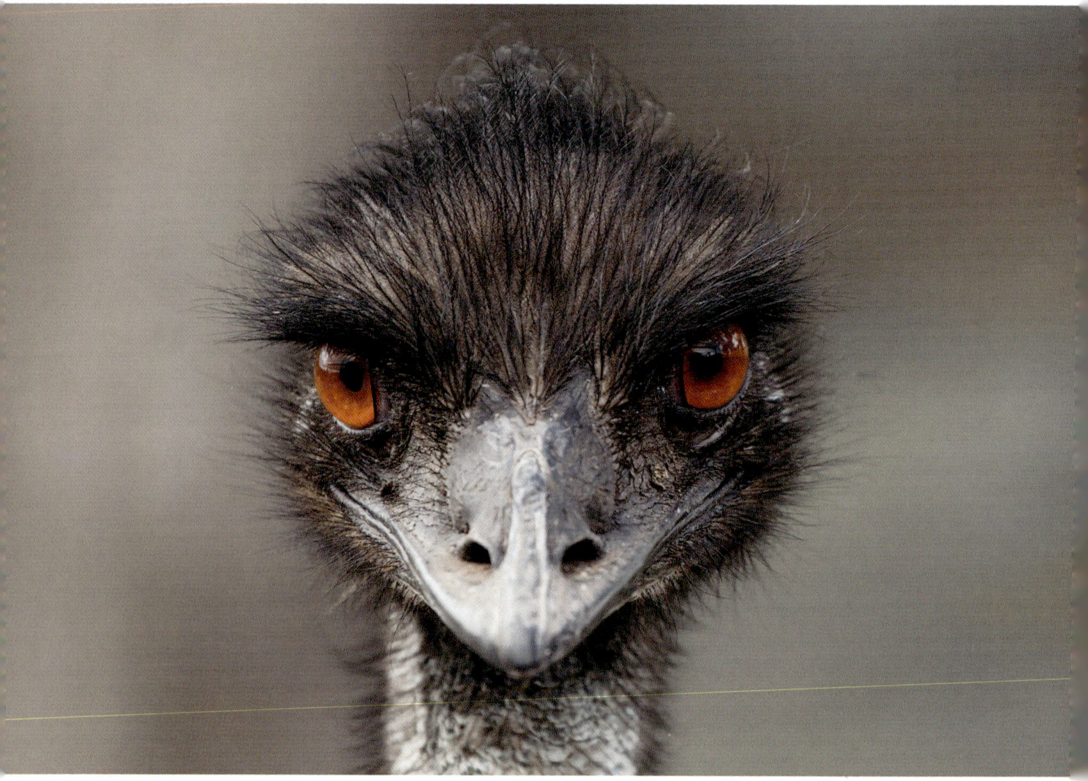

Interchangeable-lens cameras with smaller APS-C or M4/3 sensors give you a 'crop factor' advantage which can be utilised to record portrait shots like this stunning close-up of an Emu by Morgan Jackson of Toowoomba Camera House in Queensland. The APS-C sensor in the camera meant the 300mm focal length of the lens was extended to an effective focal length of 480mm which, at the aperture of f/5.6 produced soft and attractive blurring to isolate the subject from the background. Canon EOS 70D with EF 70-300mm lens at 300mm, ISO 400, 1/400 second at f/5.6. © Morgan Jackson.

Realistically, high-end, professional cameras won't suit most people because of their high prices and complexity. Better options can be found when you quantify your real requirements.

Understand your needs

Choosing the right camera generally comes down to three basic questions:

1. What kinds of pictures do you want to take?
2. What are your budget limits?
3. How will you share your images (and videos, if they're part of your requirements)?

There are some additional constraints for bird photography:

1. You must get close enough to subjects for pictures to be meaningful.
2. You often need to use the equipment hand-held so you can move about, particularly where hides aren't available.
3. The camera and lens must respond quickly when you aim at a subject.

Consider what kind of camera will be best for you, personally. While smartphones are convenient and can often achieve telephoto focal lengths, the resulting images are often degraded by JPEG artefacts and colour may be poorly reproduced.

Interchangeable-lens cameras deliver better images and provide a much wider choice of lenses. But you must decide between full-frame, APS-C or Micro Four Thirds (M4/3) formats.

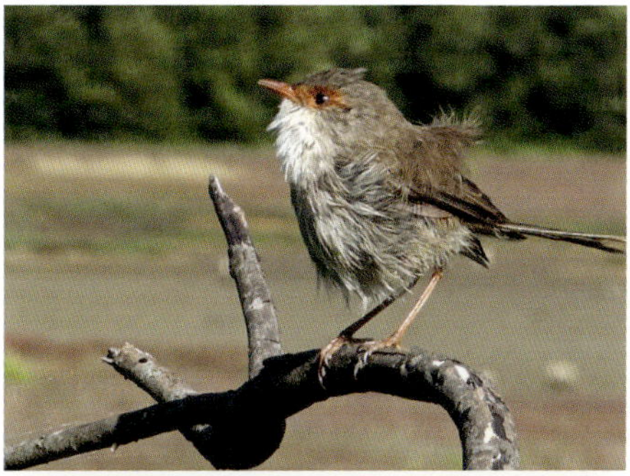

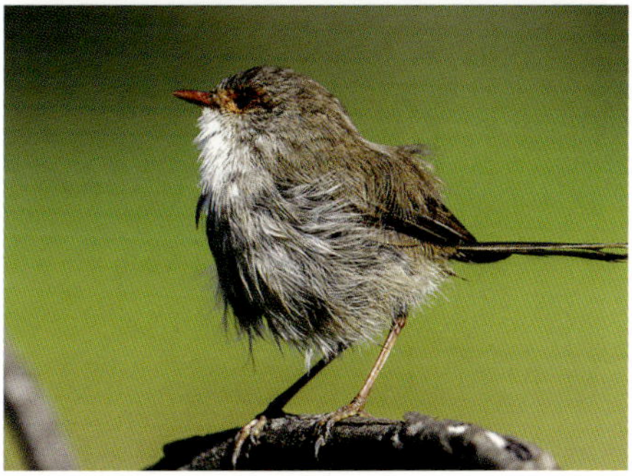

While the latest smartphones can be used for bird photography, as shown in the top picture of this Fairy Wren, they won't give you results as good as a mirrorless camera with an appropriate lens like the gear used for the lower image. Exposure details for lower image: OM-1 Mk II camera with M.Zuiko Digital ED 150-600mm f/5.0-6.3 IS lens at 600mm (1200mm equivalent in 35mm format), ISO 200, 1/640 second at f/6.3.

A full-frame camera can provide slightly better image and video quality in challenging lighting because its larger photosites can collect more light for a given resolution. However, full-frame equipment is usually larger, heavier and costlier than smaller formats.

Cameras with smaller sensors are usually smaller and lighter than full-frame models – and so are the dedicated lenses for them. They provide the advantage of a 'crop factor' that extends the effective focal length of a lens, and they may also be cheaper – depending on build quality and weather-resistance.

Cameras with APS-C sensors (measuring approximately 23.5 x 15.6 mm for Fujifilm, Nikon and Sony and 22.3 x 14.9 mm for Canon) have crop factors of 1.5x for Fujifilm, Nikon and Sony or 1.6x for Canon. So if you fit a 200mm lens to a Fujifilm, Nikon or Sony camera, the field of view you see will be the same as you'd have with a 300mm lens. (On a Canon camera, the effective focal length becomes 320mm.)

Micro Four Thirds cameras and lenses are a little smaller still, because of smaller (17.3 x 13.0mm) sensors. Many are robust and highly weather-resistant.

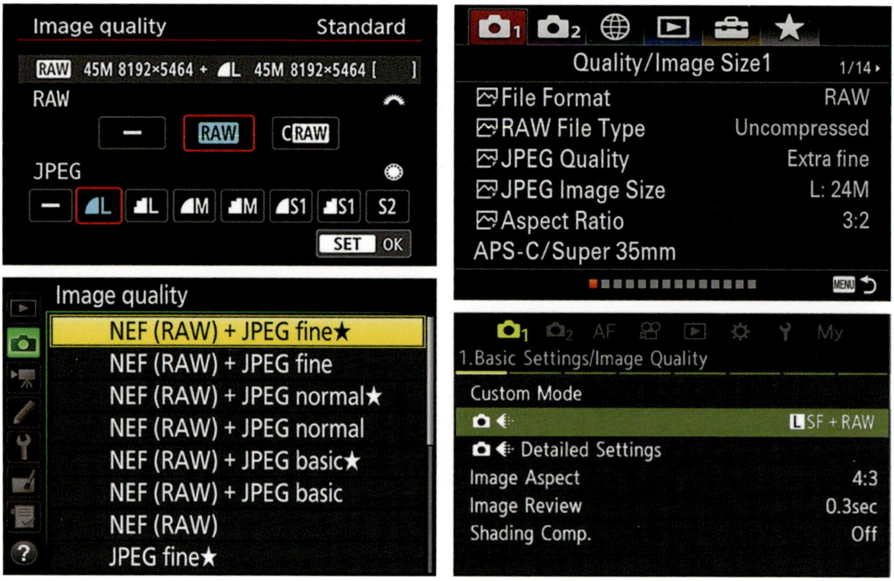

Menu settings for selecting raw file capture in four different camera brands; clockwise from top left: Canon, Sony, OM Systems, Nikon.

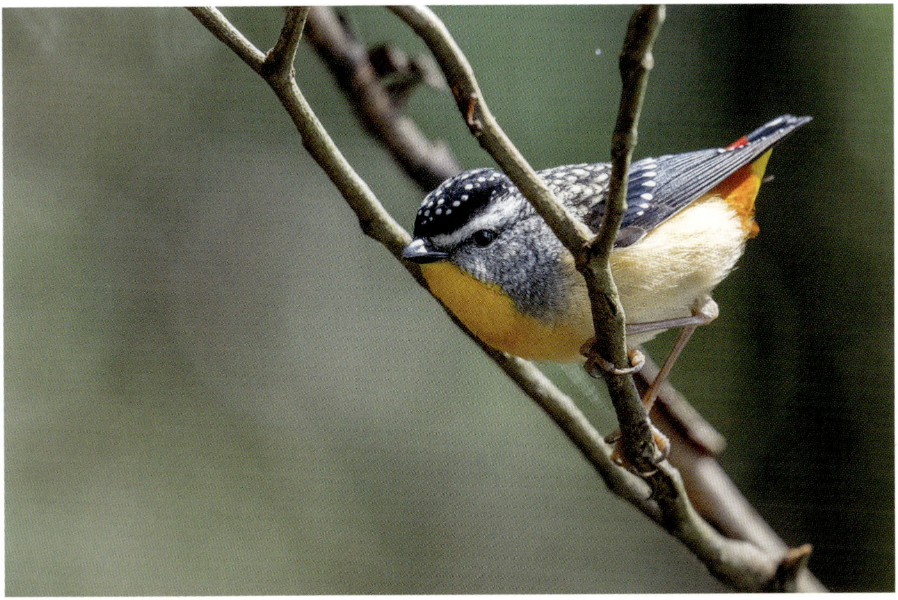

Integrated stabilisation in both the Nikon Z8 camera and Nikkor Z 180-600mm f/5.6-6.3 VR lens enabled Lachlan Cooper of Lismore Camera House to capture this great close-up portrait of a tiny Spotted Pardalote in the Border Ranges National Park in northern NSW. Exposure details: 470mm focal length, ISO 1400, 1/640 second at f/7.1. © Lachlan Cooper.

These advantages – plus the benefits of the 2x crop factor – make M4/3 equipment particularly popular with serious birders.

Camera 'must haves'

Disregard the promotional materials and focus on acquiring a camera that includes the following capabilities:

1. The ability to record raw (RAW) files – preferably at 14-bit depth. This allows you to reveal details in highlights and shadows that would normally be lost in 8-bit JPEGs and is worth having in lighting with wide (and unpredictable) brightness ranges.

2. Fast and accurate autofocusing is vital. 'Hybrid' phase- and contrast-detection systems are faster and more accurate than contrast detection alone. Your camera needs at least 100 AF points, preferably mostly 'cross-type' which can detect contrast both vertically and horizontally.

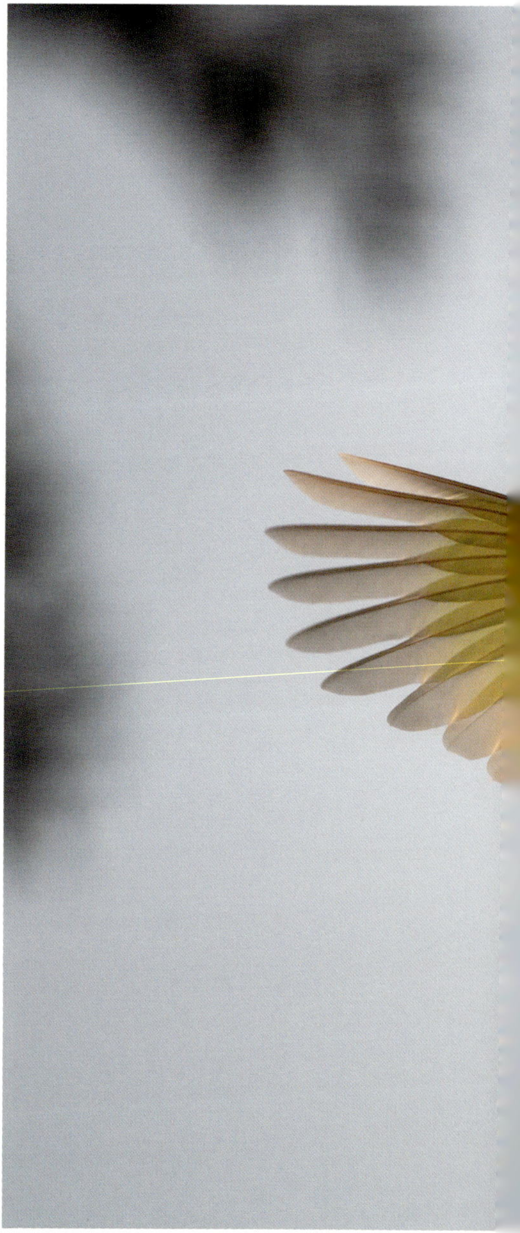

Dani Webb used a professional Nikon D5 camera and 200-500mm f/5.6 (vintage 2015) lens for this action shot of Sulphur-crested Cockatoos, taking advantage of the camera's sophisticated AF system. Exposure details: 500mm focal length, ISO 1600, 1/640 second at f/5.6. © Dani Webb.

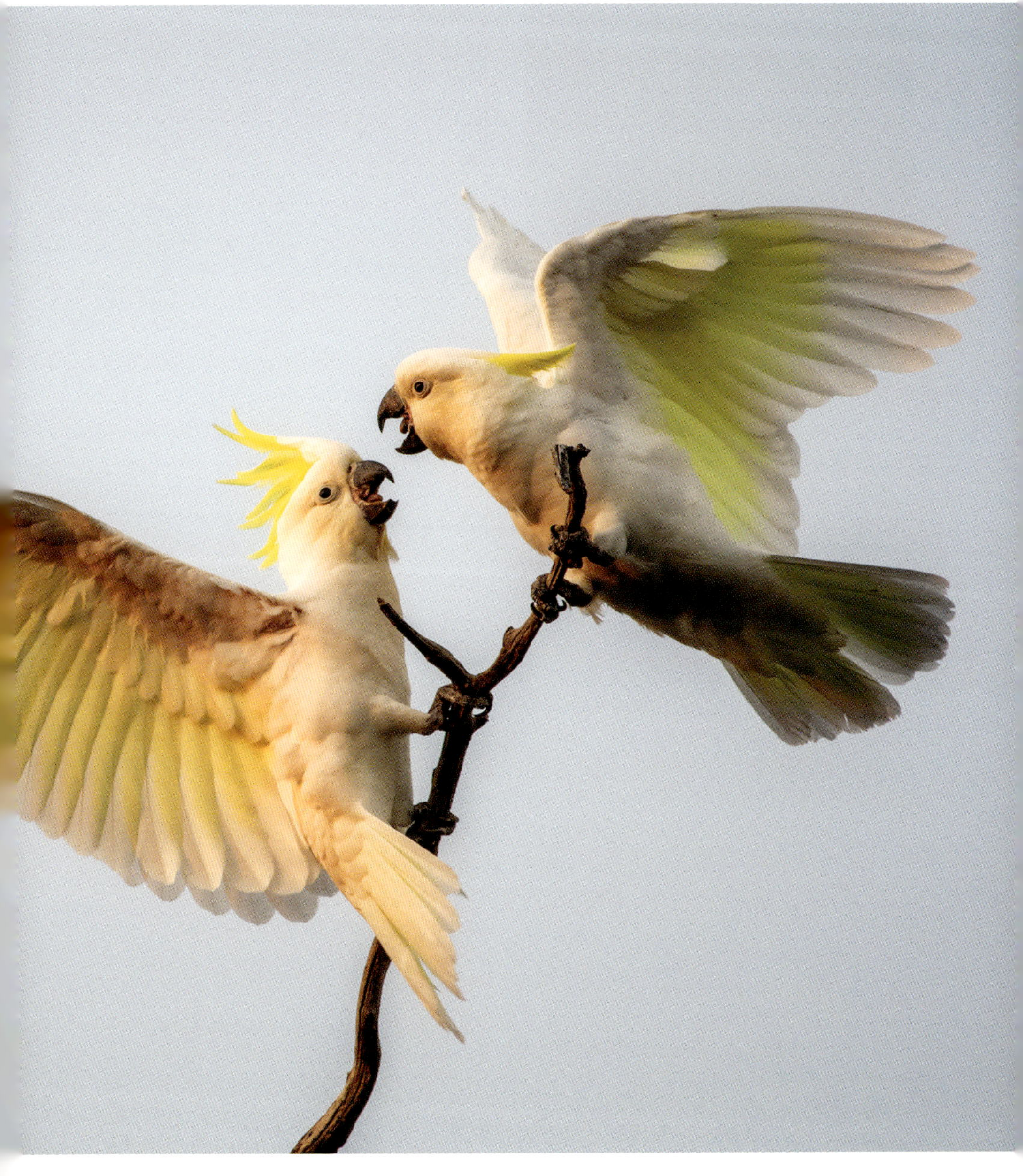

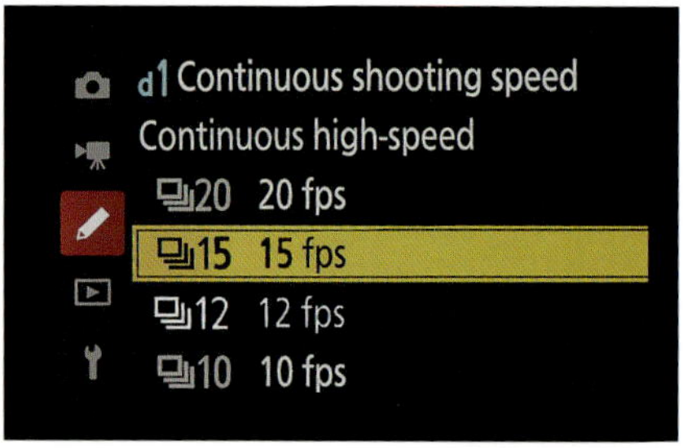

Menu settings for continuous shooting should offer a range that starts with at least 7 fps but can go as high as 20 fps for stills shooting.

The more focus points you have across the sensor, the easier it is for your camera to focus on a bird in flight. Bird detecting AF modes have a real advantage here – for both stills shooters and videographers.

3. Image stabilisation built into both the camera and lens, or IBIS (in-built image stabilisation), lets you work much more flexibly. You can shoot with the camera hand-held in challenging lighting and shift your position if your subject moves or the lighting changes. Tripods are great when you need greater steadiness, such as when you're shooting from a hide.

4. Burst shooting can be handy, although it's not always fail-safe. Cameras with pre-capture burst recording modes allow you to record frames from the time you half-press the shutter release (which activates the AF system) until the shutter button is pressed right down – and often after that. Some cameras can save up to 70 buffered images before **and** after the shutter is released.

Lens 'must haves'

Most birders recommend a telephoto lens with an effective focal length of at least 300mm to start with – but be guided by how much weight you can hold steadily. Lens speed, which comes with larger lens elements, influences the overall weight of a lens. For example, the Nikkor Z 600mm f/6.3 VR S super telephoto lens, which is classed as 'the lightest in its class' for full-frame cameras weighs almost 1.4 kilograms, while the much slower Canon RF 600mm f/11 IS STM lens weighs only 930 grams.

Zoom lenses are more versatile than prime (single focal length) lenses and often more affordable, although they may be a stop or two slower. Lenses with a constant maximum aperture maintain their 'speed' throughout their focal length range but can cost more and be heavier than lenses with variable maximum apertures.

Weight is important if you need to carry your camera for long distances; anything over two kilograms will slow you down and tire you out. It's less important when you can drive up close to a hide or photograph birds from the comfort of a vehicle. But, even then, lenses weighing more than 2.5 kg can be difficult to keep steady and should be used on a tripod.

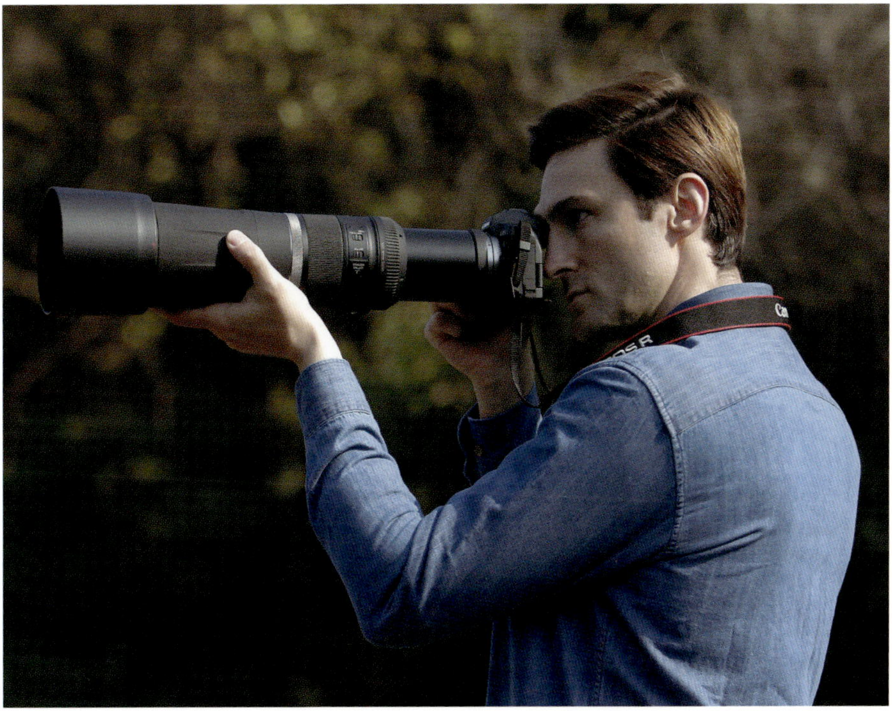

Canon's RF 800mm f/11 IS STM lens is the lightest in its class, weighing just over 1.24 kilograms, which is less than half the weight of the faster RF 800mm f/5.6 L IS USM lens, making it much easier to use for handheld shooting. (Source: Canon.)

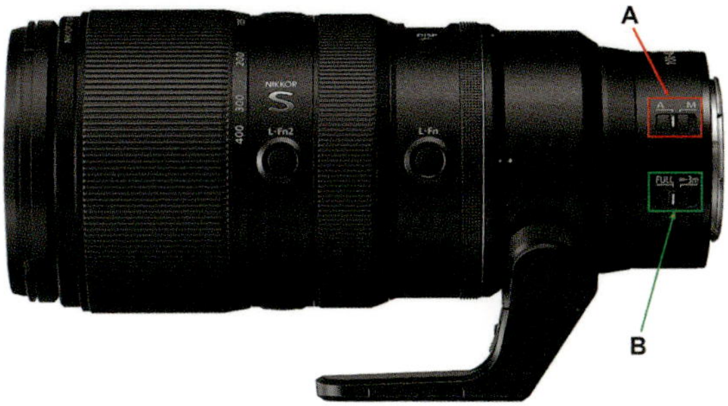

The autofocus on/off switch (A) and the focus limiter (B) on a Nikkor 100-400mm telephoto zoom lens. (Source: Nikon.)

Most telephoto lenses have slider adjustments for switching between auto and manual focus plus a focus limiter switch (to minimise back-and-forth 'hunting' for focus), as shown in the illustration on page 21. An on/off IS switch may also be included – unless stabilisation is controlled by the camera. A lens hood is another essential; don't buy a lens without one.

Teleconverters can provide a cheap way to extend the effective focal length of lenses. Most manufacturers offer 1.4x and 2x teleconverters, which increase the effective focal length of a lens by a factor of 1.4x or 2x, respectively. Find out more about them in Chapter 7.

Don't worry about...

Disregard the megapixel count. For most people, a 20-megapixel camera will be more than adequate – as long as you don't zoom by cropping. If you shoot raw files and have adequate editing skills you can print your images as large as A2 size – even if they were taken with a cropped-sensor camera.

Useful links

Choosing a lens kit
www.tinyurl.com/lens-kits

Useful accessories
www.tinyurl.com/photog-accessories

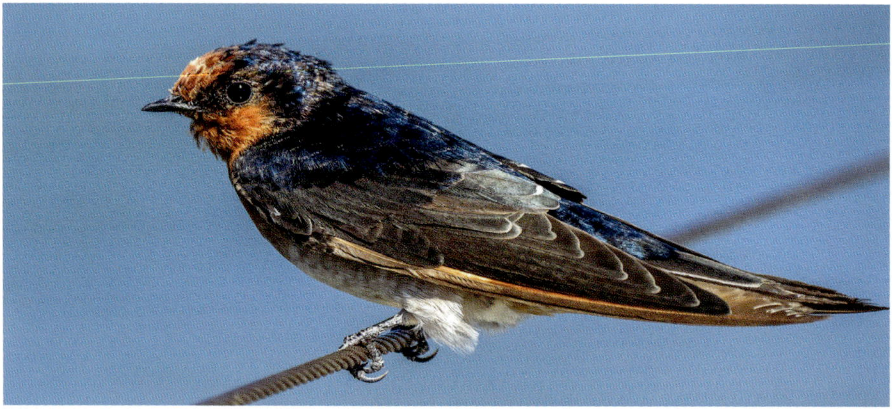

This close-up of a perched Welcome Swallow was recorded using a 16-megapixel M4/3 camera and a 400mm telephoto lens, which effectively became an 800mm lens due to the sensor's crop factor. There is enough detail recorded to print the image at A3+ (483 x 329 mm) size – or slightly larger. OM-1 camera with Panasonic Leica 100-400mm f/4-6.3 lens at 400mm, ISO 200, 1/500 second at f/7.1.

CHAPTER 3

BACKYARD BIRDS

Australians are fortunate in having plenty of native birds coming to visit our backyards, and lucky to have an organisation like Birdlife Australia to help us keep track of them. Their regular surveys help us understand how birds survive in our cities and towns and how to make our backyards more bird friendly.

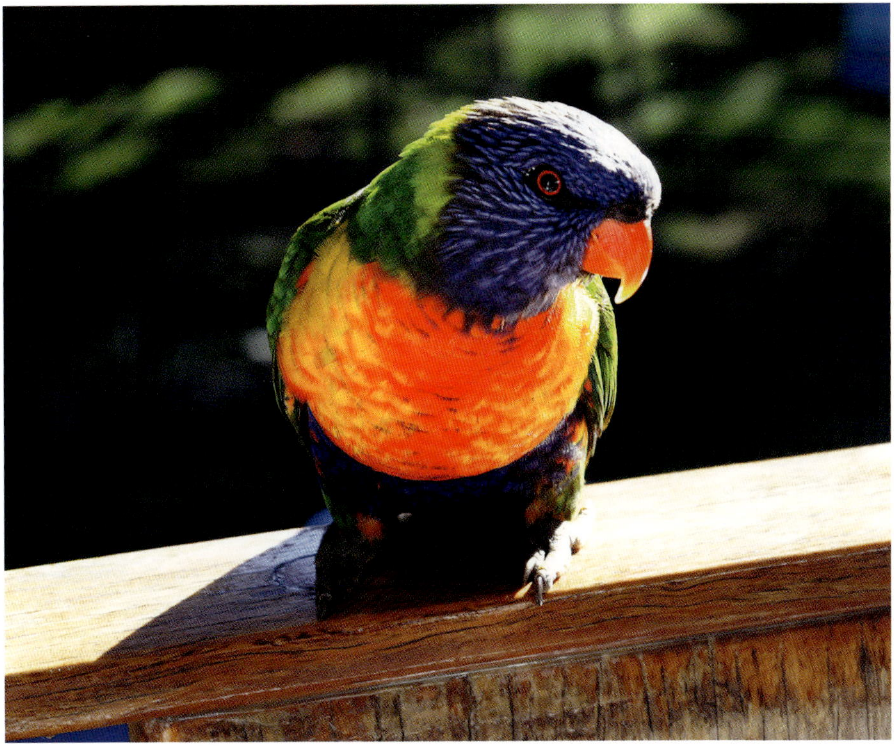

People living near parks often find common backyard birds like the Rainbow Lorikeet visit their balconies. Sony NEX-5 camera with 18-55mm f/3.5-5.6 OSS kit lens at 55mm (82.5mm in 35mm format), ISO 200, 1/100 second at f/7.1.

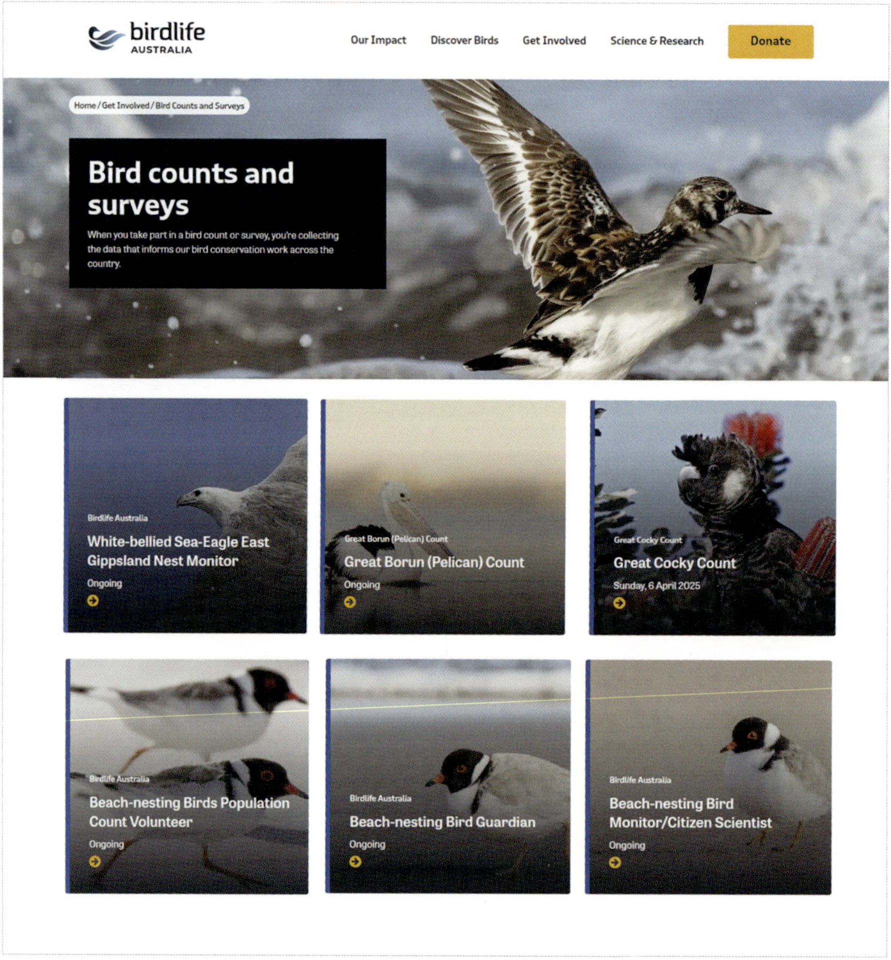

Bird lovers all round Australia can be 'citizen scientists' by joining one of Birdlife Australia's monitoring groups, which help to safeguard our native birds. (Source: Birdlife Australia.)

Four Birds in Backyards Seasonal Surveys (www.tinyurl.com/bird-counts) take place across the year, one for each of the seasons:

- Autumn (March and April)
- Winter (June and July)
- Spring (September and October)
- Summer (December and January)

Even people without backyards can take part; any location near your home where you can see birds is fine, such as a local park or school. The data you collect helps research into bird numbers, their behaviour, what features of our gardens they like and what they avoid.

You don't need expert knowledge to participate. The survey forms show you how to identify common birds while prize draws are conducted to incentivise participants to complete at least one survey per season.

Common backyard birds

The 2024 Summer Birds in Backyards survey recorded 271 species in a total of 26,335 birds. The 10 most frequently-recorded species are listed in the table below, along with the percentage of surveys in which that species was seen (reporting rate).

This list changes with changing seasons. 'Urban adapters' like Rainbow Lorikeets and Magpie Larks are regularly among the most reported birds throughout the year, as are the deliberately introduced Spotted Dove and Common Myna. Eastern Koels are only seen in the summer months when they migrate south from tropical Australia and Indonesia.

Climatic variations and the availability of food resources determine where different species are found. The CSIRO lists the following species as the top five species for each state and territory as follows:

Australian Capital Territory: Australian Magpie, Magpie-lark, Pied Currawong, Crimson Rosella, Red Wattlebird.

New South Wales: Australian Magpie, Magpie-lark, Superb Fairy-wren, Australian Raven, Laughing Kookaburra.

Common Name	**Reporting Rate**
Rainbow Lorikeet	43%
Magpie-lark	33%
Australian Magpie	31%
Sulphur-crested Cockatoo	26%
Willie Wagtail	26%
Noisy Miner	25%
Common Myna	23%
Galah	22%
Spotted Dove	21%
Eastern Koel	21%

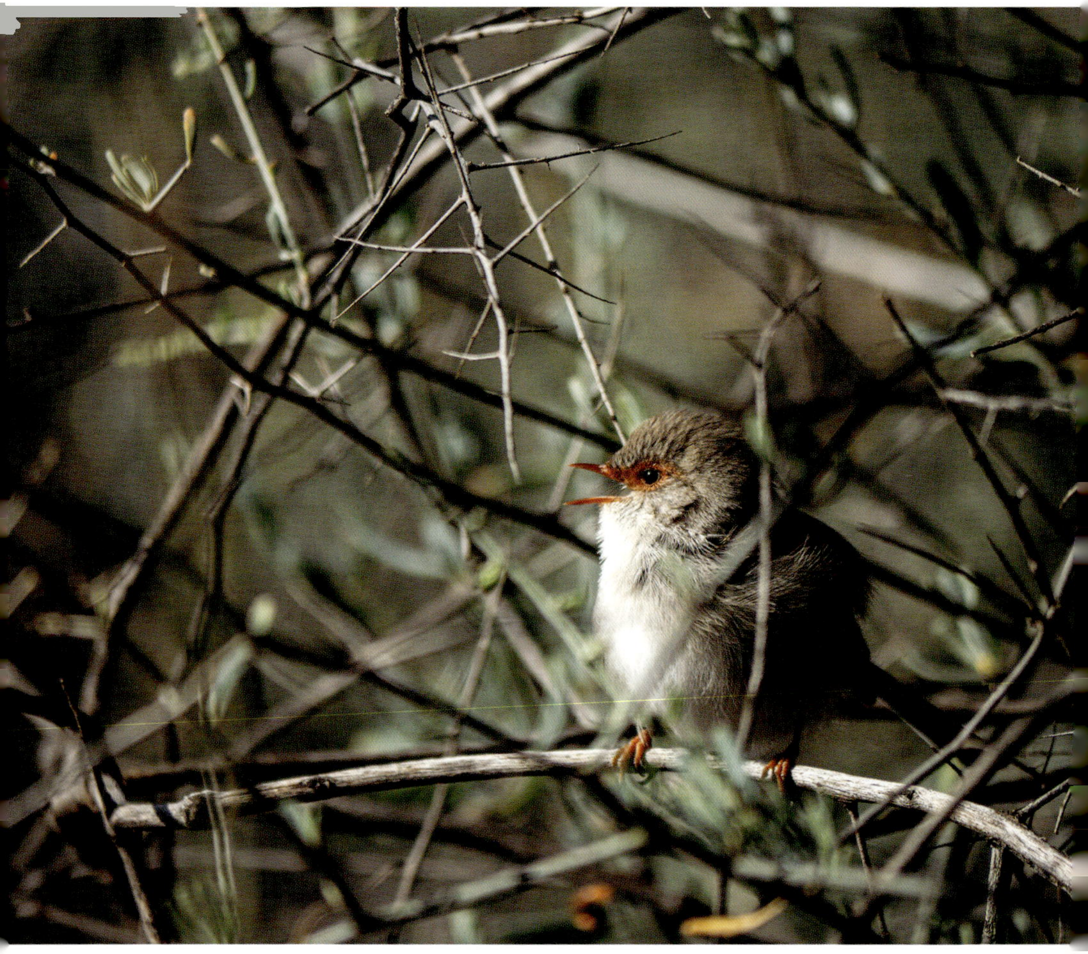

Smaller birds like this female Superb Fairy-wren require dense vegetation for protection against predators and larger aggressive birds. OM-D E-M1 II camera with Panasonic Lumix G Vario 100-300mm f/4-5.6 lens at 300mm focal length (600mm equivalent in 35mm format), ISO 200, 1/640 second at f/5.6.

Northern Territory: Magpie Goose, Magpie-lark, Willie Wagtail, Bar-shouldered Dove, Rainbow Bee-eater.

Queensland: Torresian Crow, Magpie-lark, Australian Magpie, Willie Wagtail, Masked Lapwing.

South Australia: Australian Magpie, Galah, Willie Wagtail, New Holland Honeyeater, Red Wattlebird.

Tasmania: Forest Raven, Superb Fairy-wren, Masked Lapwing, Grey Fantail, Common blackbird.

Victoria: Australian Magpie, Red Wattlebird, Superb Fairy-wren, Magpie-lark, Little Raven.

Western Australia: Willie Wagtail, Australian Raven, Australian Magpie, Magpie-lark, Australian Ringneck.

Attracting birds

Birdlife Australia provides the following advice on attracting birds to your garden:

1. Plants that grow naturally in your area provide the right food and shelter for local native birds, unlike some hybrids or plants from other parts of Australia. They're also less likely to become weeds in adjacent bushland areas. If you can't get locally native plants, other natives are the next best thing.

2. Plant a mixture of species to ensure you have different plants flowering, fruiting and seeding throughout the year.

3. Select plants that will provide a complex vertical structure from the ground up, including groundcovers such as grasses or ferns, small and medium-sized shrubs plus a couple of trees (if you have space). Smaller birds need dense vegetation to nest in and also to hide from larger, aggressive or carnivorous birds.

4. Reduce the area of lawn. Large areas of lawn mainly attract common and often aggressive birds.

5. Water is important for making your garden bird-friendly. Fresh water can be provided in a bird bath, hollowed boulders or a garden pond.

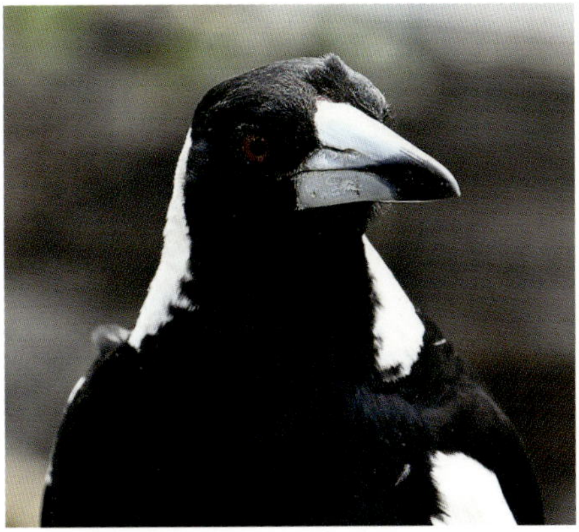

Australian Magpies are common and found wherever there is a combination of trees and adjacent open areas. They live in groups of up to 24 birds and feed mostly on the ground, searching for insects and their larvae. Nikon Z 50 camera with Nikkor Z DX 18-140mm f/3.5-6.3 VR lens at 140mm, ISO 800, 1/80 second at f/6.3, Aperture-priority AE mode with centre-weighted metering.

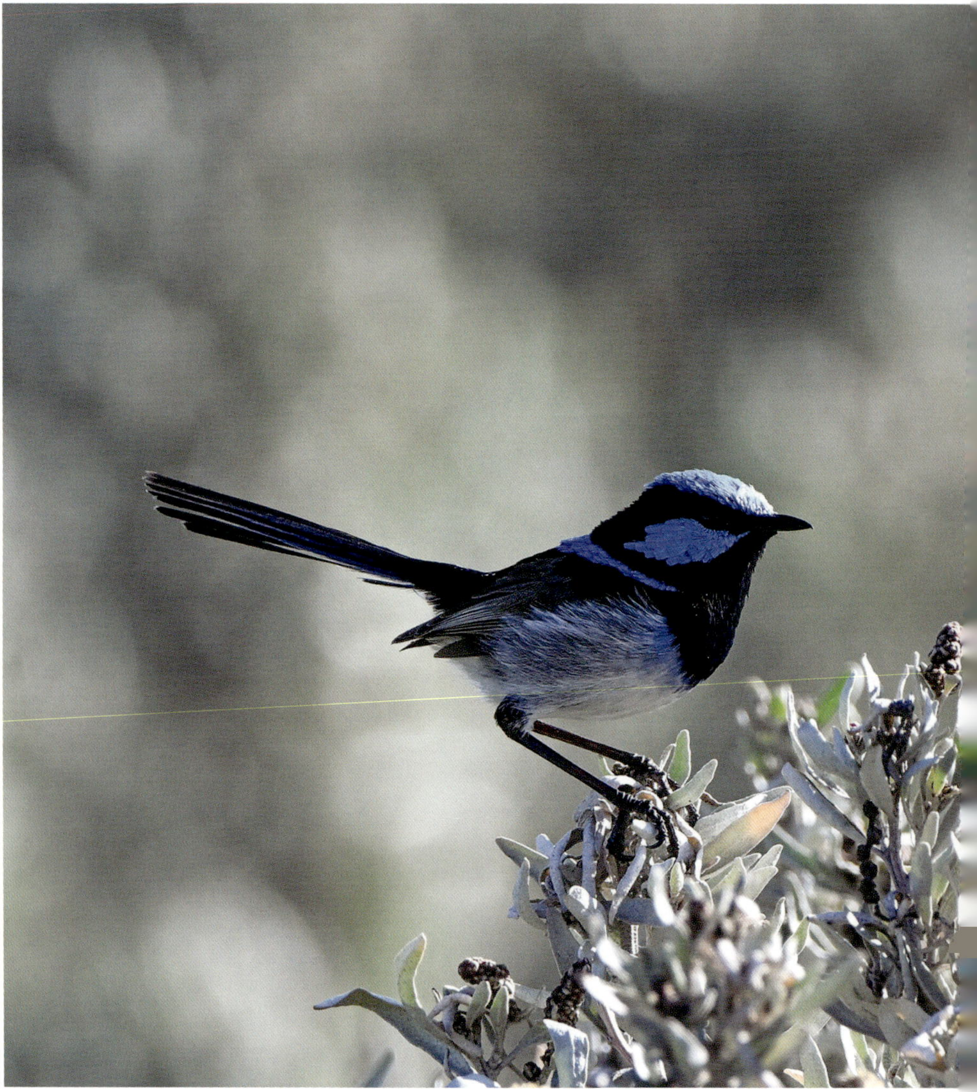

Superb Fairy-wrens like this one photographed by Dani Webb visit many gardens in NSW, Victoria and Tasmania. Nikon Z 8 camera with AF-S Nikkor 200-500mm f/5.6E ED VR lens at 500mm, ISO 400 1/1250 second at f/5.6.

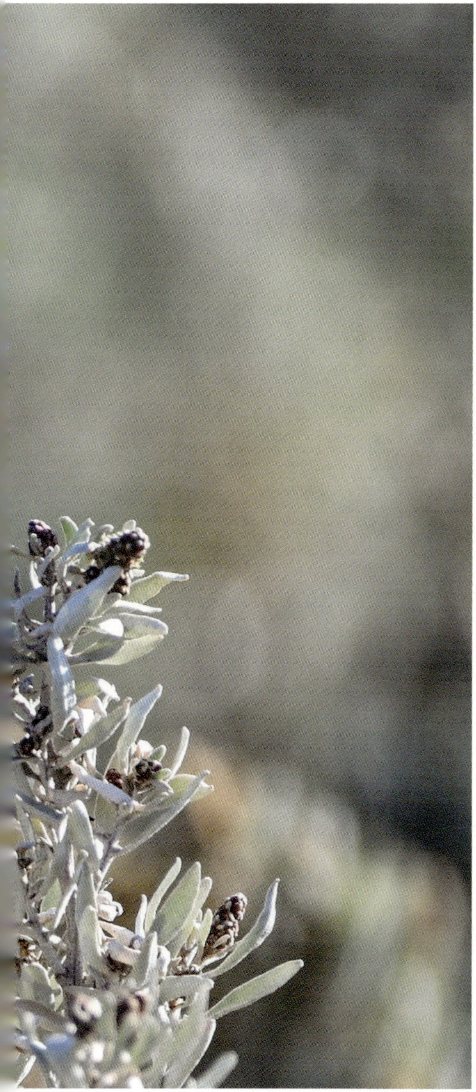

6. Avoid sprays and chemicals unless you really need them. Using a chemical may solve one problem but often creates another, such as toxic run-off. Birds are the best way to keep your plant-eating insects in check. Only use low-phosphorus fertilisers especially formulated for Australian native plants or mulch instead.

7. Safeguard birds from pets. According to the Threatened Species HUB, pet cats kill on average 186 mammals, birds and reptiles in a year – so keep your cat indoors. It's safer for cats, too, and they'll enjoy longer and healthier lives.

Many local councils provide guides for planting indigenous plants in your garden, which can help attract native birds.

To feed or not?

Bird feeders are a contentious issue as they can disrupt population balances and make some birds so dependent they risk starvation if you go away for any length of time. Only provide supplemental feeding when natural resources aren't available.

It's better to have a range of native plants that produce seeds, nectar and/or attract insects throughout the year and provide a needed food resource during high-demand periods like the breeding season. This also enables young fledglings to learn how to find naturally occurring foods.

There's no reason you shouldn't provide the occasional snack for the birds that come to your door. Most Australian birds live long lives and have relatively large brains compared to their European counterparts so they can cope with feast and famine conditions in the Australian environment.

Many common species are also nomadic, semi-nomadic or seasonally migratory and can easily adapt and switch between diets. Those that aren't are usually restricted to one territory.

One item you can provide is a bird bath. In a dry continent like Australia, bird baths provide vital support when there's a risk of heat stress. They are also places where birds can socialise, clean their feathers and find refuge if they are disturbed.

Always place the bird bath out of the reach of cats and other predators. Keep it filled and make sure the water remains clean – including in winter. A dirty bath can spread disease, when many birds congregate to bathe and drink.

Useful links

Bird-friendly garden tips
www.tinyurl.com/bird-friendly-garden

Birds in backyards
www.birdsinbackyards.net

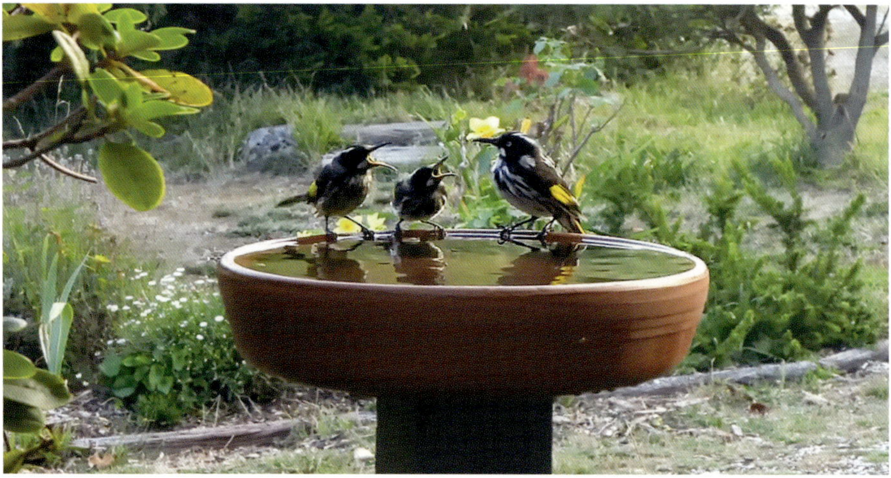

Installing a bird bath in your garden is one of the best ways to attract birds like these New Holland Honeyeaters all year round. (Image from smartphone video.)

Problem species

What do you do when the birds in your garden are not the birds you want? They may be introduced species like Common Mynas, Starlings, Blackbirds and feral Pigeons or native species such as Noisy Miners, Pied Currawongs, Sulphur-crested Cockatoos, and Brush-turkeys.

Smaller birds can be hard to deter but many of the introduced species prefer tidy lawns, manicured hedges and hard surface areas. Creating a more bush-like native garden can help keep them away.

Netting fruit trees before the fruit starts to ripen keeps fruit eaters from damaging crops. Chicken wire or other mesh materials can cover shrubs and bushes to prevent some birds from nesting. If you hang pairs of colourful balls on trees in your garden, some birds see them as 'eyes' and try to avoid them.

Shiny reflective objects like old CDs, aluminium foil, small mirrors or even metallic wrapping paper in bushes can also deter smaller problematic birds. Larger birds like Sulphur-crested Cockatoos can be discouraged by

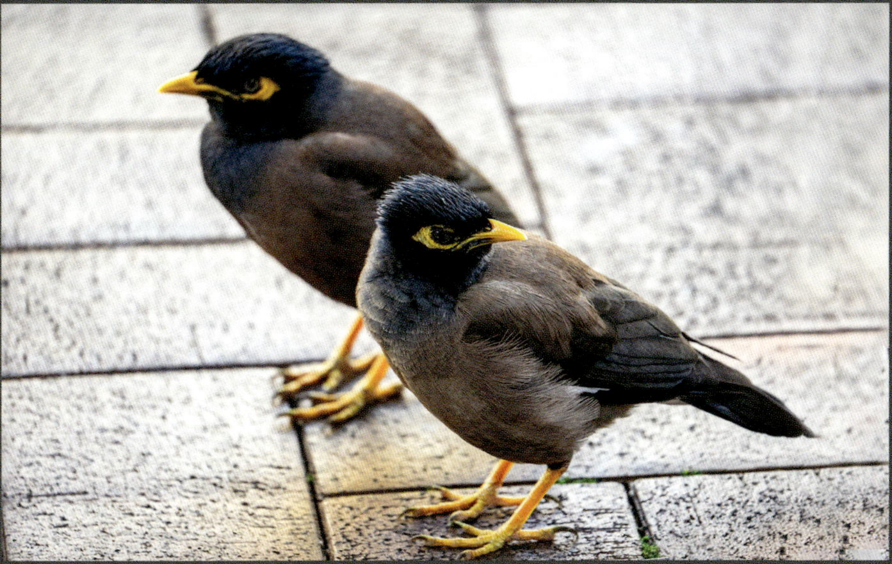

Pest species like the Common Mynas shown here prefer hard surface areas and open spaces to bush gardens. Sony ILCE-7M2 camera with Tamron 50-300mm f/4.5-6.3 Di III VC VXD lens at 300mm, ISO 2500, 1/320 second at f/6.3.

spikes on window sills and overhangs. Removing pet food and covering compost bins will dissuade scavenging species.

Brush-turkeys are mainly a problem between May and August, when the males build a mound in which to incubate eggs. During this period they scrape up large quantities of leaves, twigs and grass and can completely re-landscape a suburban garden.

Although not endangered, Brush-turkeys are protected. Relocating one from your garden is difficult since they usually come back or are quickly replaced by another turkey. Physically destroying the mound won't work as the turkey will simply start again. The best approach is to cover vulnerable areas with wire mesh to stop them from scratching.

If you can leave the turkey to display his natural behaviour you'll be rewarded with an excellent subject for your camera. Once the mound is built, the turkey will re-use it in subsequent years and his need to destroy your garden is often reduced. On the plus side, Brush-turkeys are very good at keeping garden bugs under control.

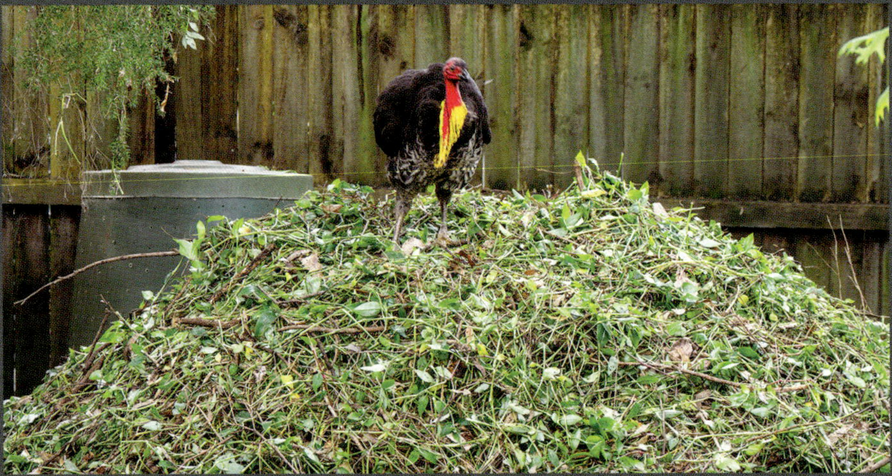

Brush-turkeys are found from the Cape York Peninsula, south through suburban Sydney to the Illawarra region of NSW. In the breeding season, males scratch debris from a radius of about 20 metres to create a mound that can be 4 metres in diameter and up to 1.5 metres high. OM-D EM-1 Mark II camera with M. Zuiko Digital ED 12-100mm f4.0 IS PRO lens at 57mm (114mm in 35mm equivalent), ISO 200, 1/40 second at f/4.5.

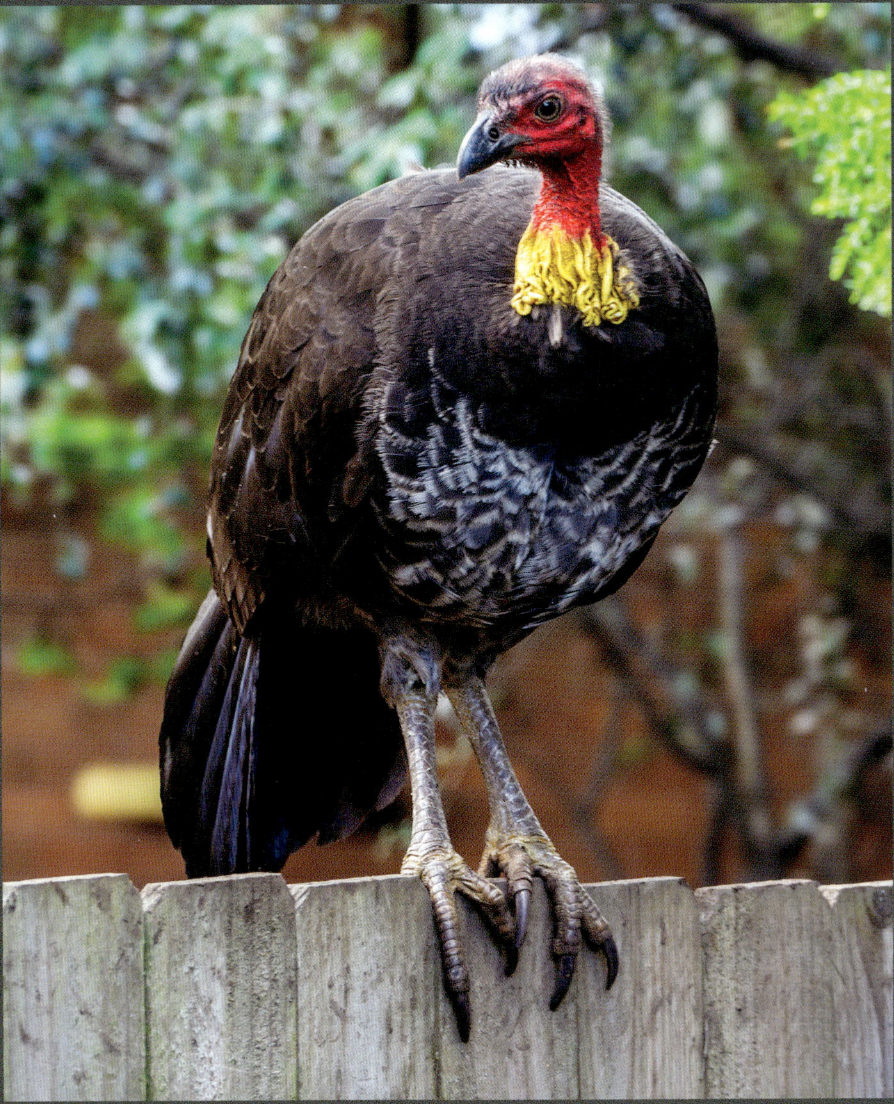

If you can tolerate an Australian Brush-turkey you'll find he provides plenty of photo opportunities. EM-1 Mark II camera with M. Zuiko Digital ED 12-100mm f4.0 IS PRO lens at 100mm (200mm in 35mm equivalent), ISO 800, 1/25 second at f/6.3.

CHAPTER 4

BEST LOCATIONS AROUND AUSTRALIA

A state-by-state guide to some of the best places for bird watching in Australia.

Australian Capital Territory

The territory's top bird-watching sites are the Jerrabomberra Wetlands, Mulligans Flat Woodland Sanctuary, the Namadgi National Park and the Tharwa Sandwash on the Murrumbidgee River (www.tinyurl.com/act-birds).

New South Wales

NSW National Parks and Wildlife Service runs bird-watching tours that range from half-day workshops to 17-day birding adventures (www.tinyurl.com/birds-nsw-parks).

Bicentennial Park in Sydney includes a Waterbird Refuge where large flocks of migrating birds come to feed in spring and summer, joining the resident Black-

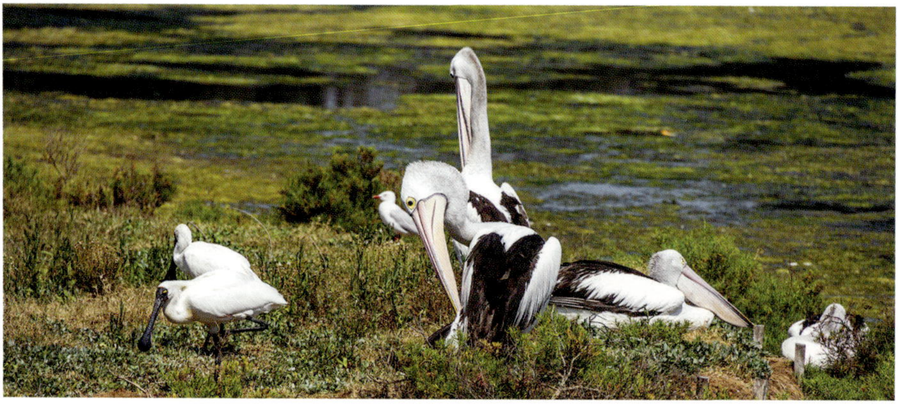

Australian Pelicans and Royal Spoonbills are among the birds that make their homes in the wetlands of the Waterbird Refuge in Sydney's Bicentennial Park. Canon EOS RP camera with RF 24-240mm f/4-6.3 IS USM lens at 240mm; ISO 100, 1/800 second at f/6.3; Aperture-priority AE, centre-weighted metering.

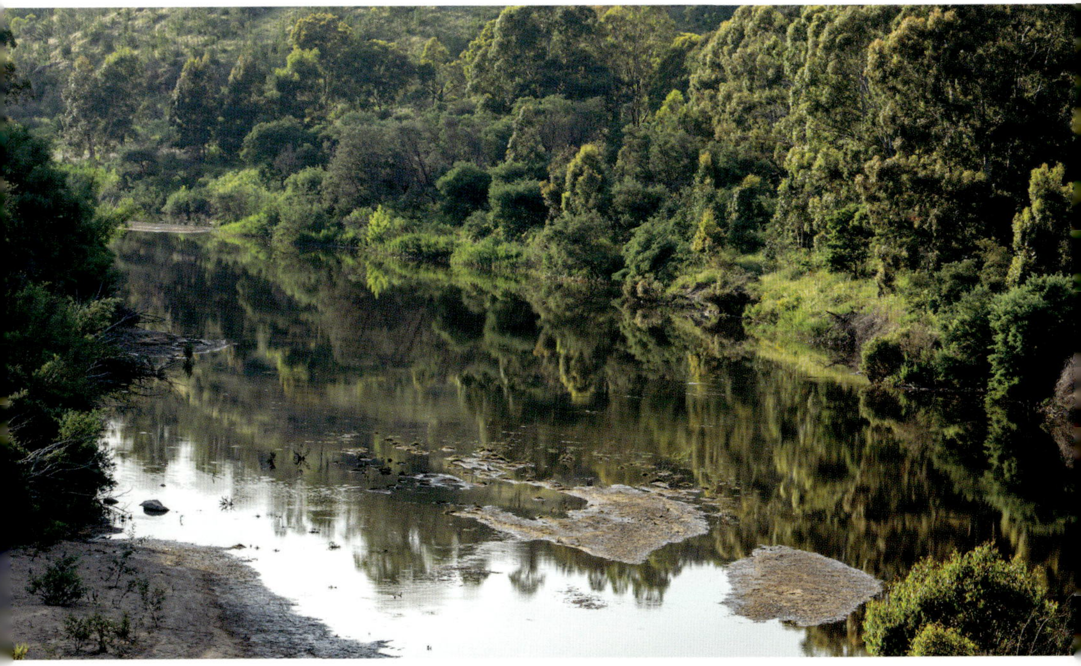

The Tharwa Sandwash on the Murrumbidgee River is a well-known hotspot for seeing large numbers of honeyeaters in the autumn. Canon EOS 7D Mark II with EF 100-400mm f/4.5-5.6L IS II USM lens at 100mm; ISO 100, 1/100 second at f/10, spot metering. (Source: Camera House.)

winged Stilts, Black Swans, Grey Teals, Australian Pelicans and Spoonbills.

Blue Mountains National Park includes sites covering parks and gardens, woodlands, dry and moist forest, escarpment heaths as well as freshwater wetlands (www.tinyurl.com/birds-bm and www.tinyurl.com/birds-bm2).

Capertee Valley near Lithgow is an important breeding ground for the beautiful and endangered Regent Honeyeater (www.tinyurl.com/capertee).

The rainforest in **Dorrigo National Park** comes alive with birdlife during spring. Learn more through this self-guided audio tour: www.tinyurl.com/dorrigo-birds.

Lord Howe Island is home to a seabird breeding frenzy over summer as well as several other endemic species (www.lordhoweisland.info/experiences).

The Wombeyan Karst Conservation Reserve is a great place to photograph Gang-gang Cockatoos (www.tinyurl.com/wombeyan).

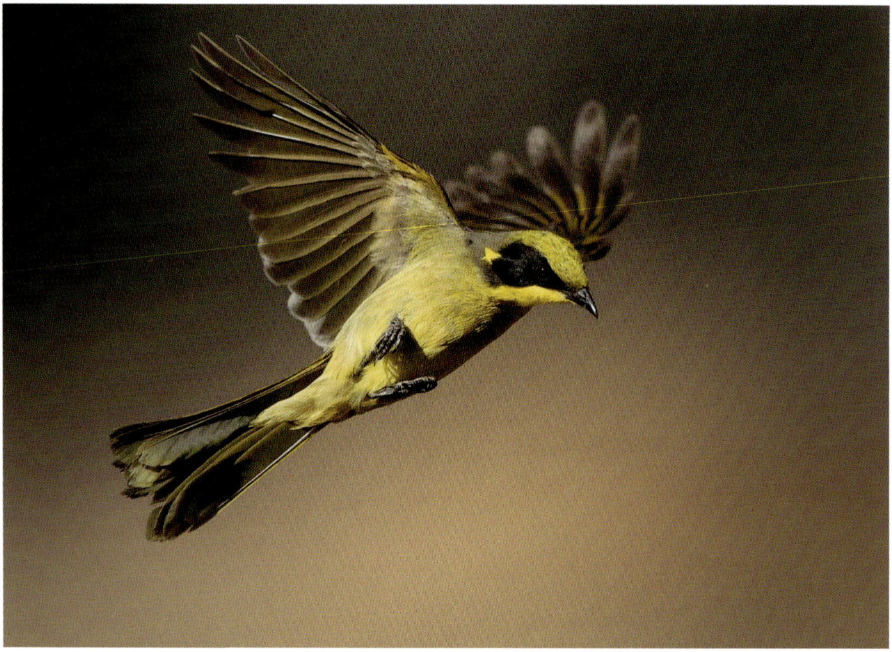

Yellow-tufted honeyeater (Lichenostomus melanops) at Glen Alice near Lithgow. © JJ Harrison (www.jjharrison.com.au), accessed under the Creative Commons Attribution-Share Alike 4.0 International license.

The Menindee Lakes in the far west attracts more than 220 species of birdlife, including large flocks of Black Swans, Budgerigars, Pelicans, Major Mitchell Cockatoos and Emus (www.menindeelakes.com).

The Macquarie Marshes in central north-west NSW is a Ramsar-listed area renowned for large numbers of water birds and migratory waders (www.tinyurl.com/mac-marshes).

Yanga National Park, which is situated beside the Murrumbidgee River near Balranald in south-western NSW. The park is home to more than 150 species of birds and includes scenic wetland views and family friendly walking tracks (www.tinyurl.com/yanga-np).

Northern Territory

The best time of year to visit is during the dry season between May and September.

The **Darwin** region is a birdwatcher's paradise, with many locations within a 100-kilometre drive (www.tinyurl.com/darwin-birds).

The numerous birdwatching trails in the **Alice Springs** area are outlined in a downloadable leaflet (www.tinyurl.com/alice-birds).

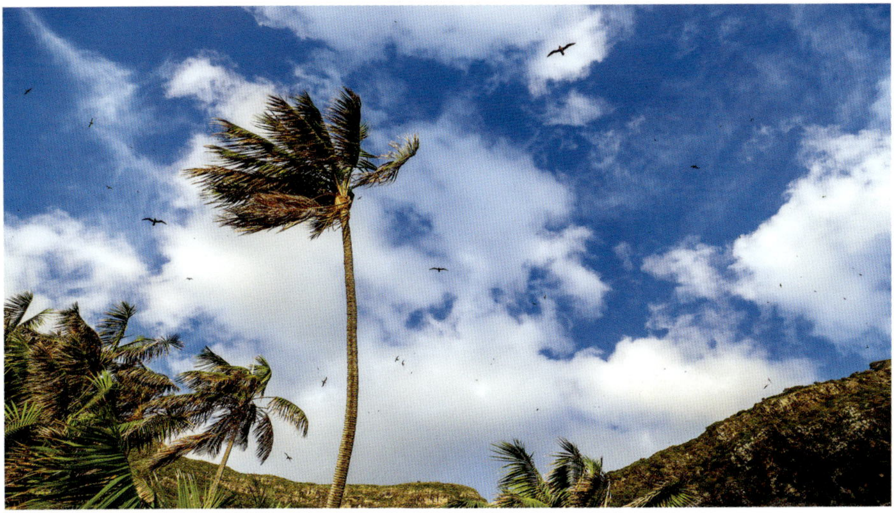

Lord Howe Island off the coast of NSW attracts a host of seabirds during the breeding season in summer. OM-1 Mark II camera with M. Zuiko Digital ED 12-100mm f/4.0 IS PRO lens at 12mm focal length, ISO 200, 1/800 second at f/4.5, Shutter priority AE, multi-pattern metering.

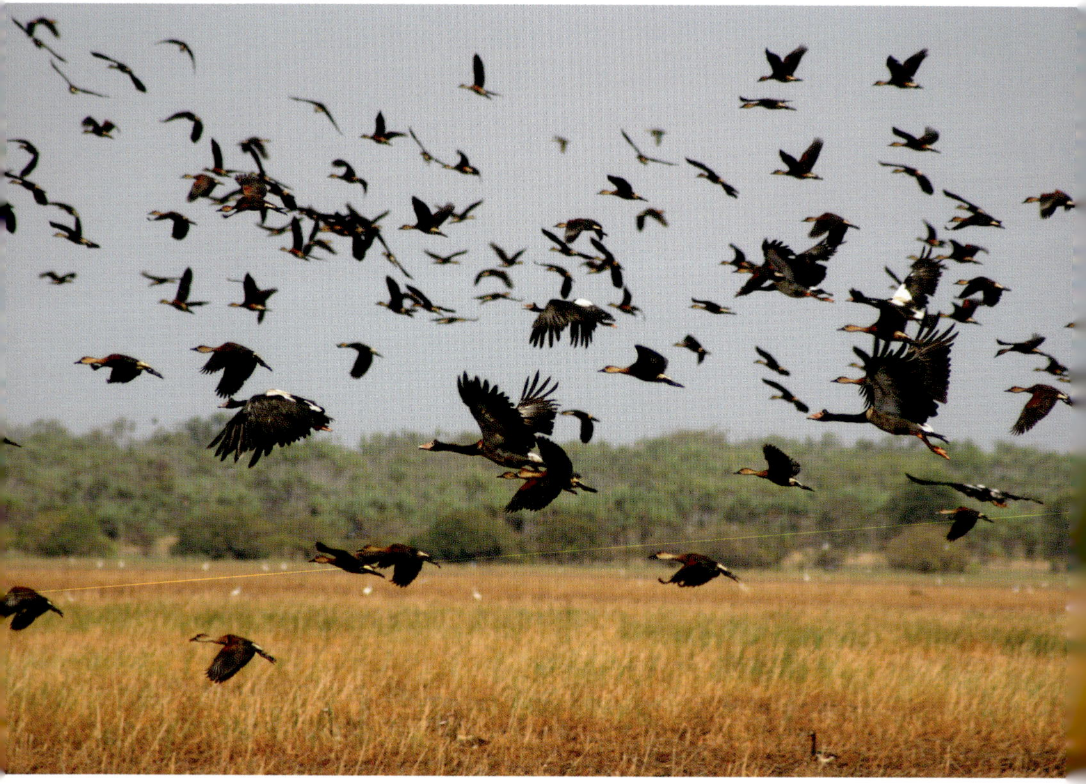

Migrating Magpie Geese and Burdekin Ducks fill the sky above the wetlands in Kakadu National Park. Canon EOS 300D camera (2006 vintage) with 300mm lens focal length, ISO 100, 1/500 second at f/6.3, multi-pattern metering. (Source: Camera House.)

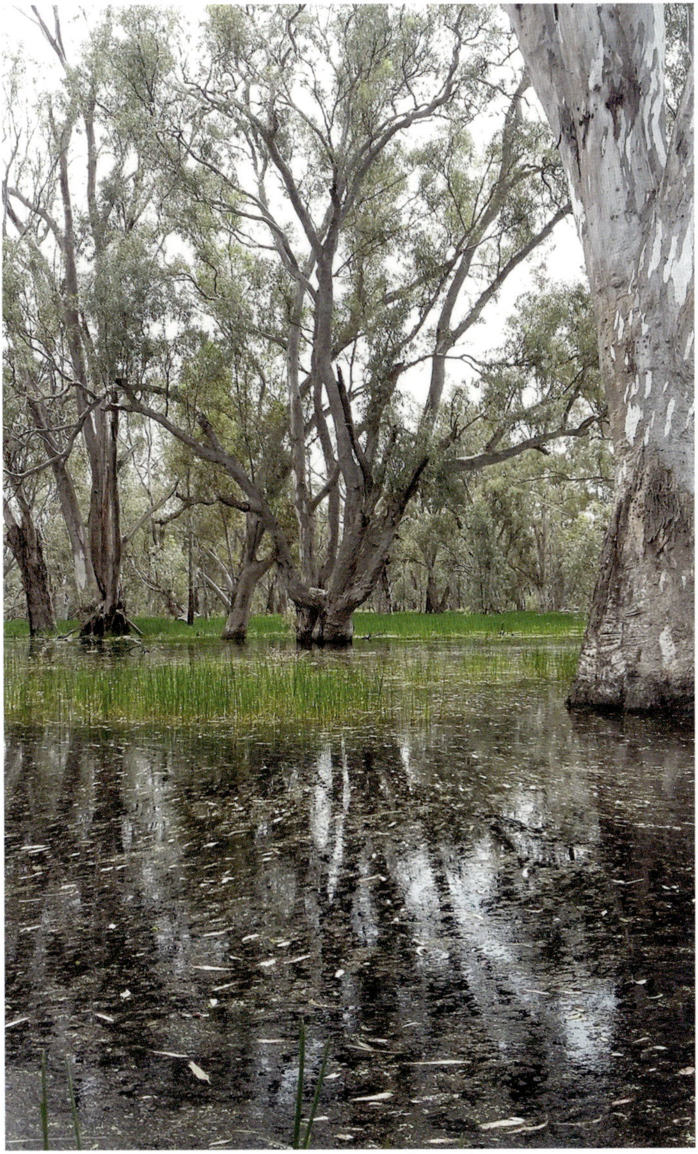

There are plenty of opportunities for birdwatching in Yanga National Park in south-western NSW. © Simone Carmichael/DCCEEW.

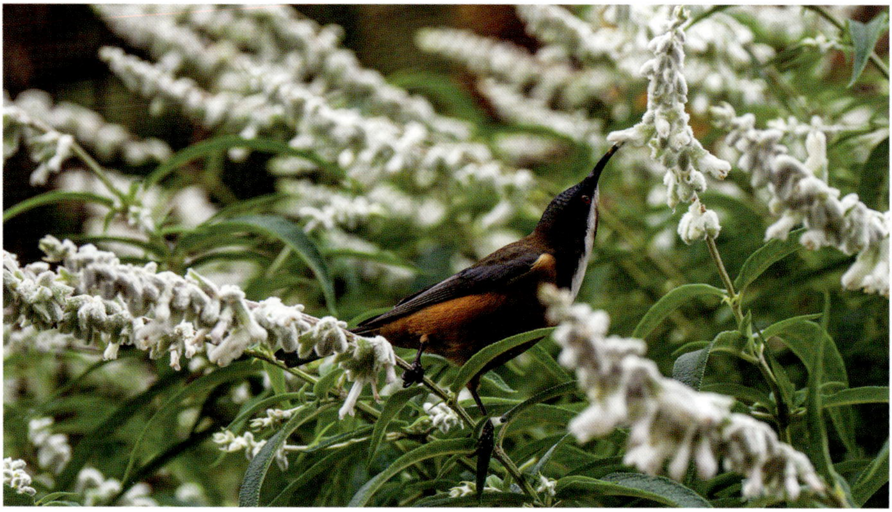

A male Eastern Spinebill foraging in shrubs, photographed at the Wittunga Botanic Garden near Blackwood. OM-1 Mark II camera with M. Zuiko Digital ED 12-100mm f/4.0 IS PRO lens at 12mm focal length, ISO 200, 1/800 second at f/4.5, Shutter priority AE, multi-pattern metering.

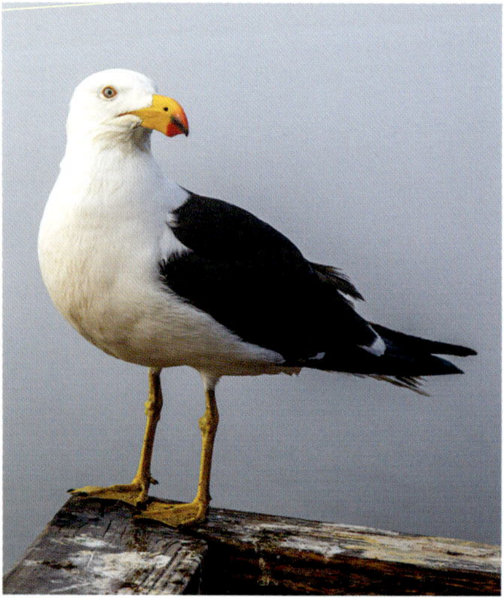

Kangaroo Island is a great place to photograph Pacific Gulls, which are easy to approach, even with modest equipment. As well as coastal habitats, the island includes large areas of unspoiled bush, which are recovering from the 2019-2020 bushfires. Canon EOS 5D camera with EF 24-105mm f/4L IS USM lens at 88mm focal length, ISO 200, 1/320 second at f/9; Aperture-priority AE, multi-pattern metering.

Kakadu National Park is home to one third of Australia's bird species, with at least 60 species found in the wetlands alone (www.tinyurl.com/kakadu-birds). Bird week tours are conducted between late September and early October at the peak of the season (www.tinyurl.com/kakadu-birds2).

Arnhem Land also hosts a bird week event at the Arnhemland Barramundi Nature Lodge (www.tinyurl.com/arnhem-birds).

The **Katherine** region's diverse landscapes are a top birding destination for seeing the vulnerable Gouldian Finch, Black-Tailed Treecreeper and Blue-Winged Kookaburra (www.tinyurl.com/katherine-birds).

Tennant Creek and the **Davenport Ranges** contain a diverse collection of waterbirds as well as honeyeaters and raptors (www.tinyurl.com/tennant-birds).

Queensland

Birds Queensland maintains a list of good bird-watching places in Queensland. It's in two parts, one covering **South-east Queensland** (www.tinyurl.com/seq-birds) south to the border, west to Inglewood, and north to Landsborough. The second part covers other sites in Queensland (www.tinyurl.com/qld-birds). Some of the sites have clickable links which should provide more detail.

Tropical North Queensland and the **Wet Tropics Rainforest** draw birders from around the world in search of the elusive Southern Cassowary of which there are believed to be only 4000 left in the wild. You have a good chance of spotting them in places like the Girringun National Park near Ingham, Barron Falls National Park in Kuranda and in the rainforests of Daintree and Cape Tribulation (www.tinyurl.com/nq-cassowary).

The **Atherton Tablelands** provides a range of Wet Tropics habitats from rainforest to wetland, volcanic lakes and open woodland (www.tinyurl.com/atherton-birds).

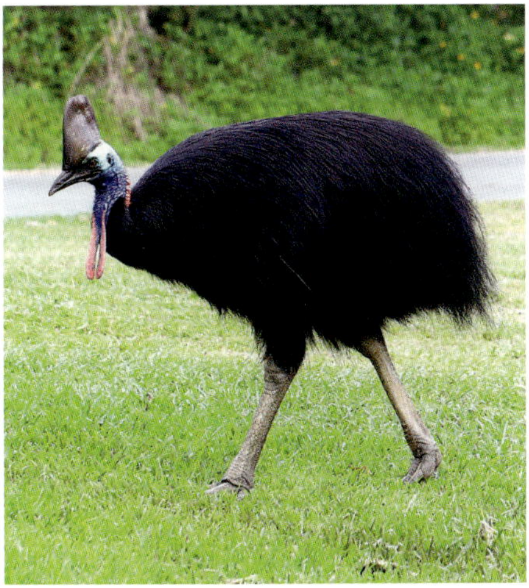

A free ranging Southern Cassowary (Casuarius casuarius) at Etty Bay, North Queensland. (Source: Graham Winterflood; accessed via the Creative Commons Attribution-ShareAlike License 4.0 on Wikipedia.)

South Australia

Adelaide's International Bird Sanctuary – Winaityinaityi Pangkara – has five main locations. Magazine Road Wetlands is a 25-minute drive from Adelaide on the northern side of the Salisbury Highway/ Port River Expressway sits the **Magazine Road Wetlands**. Whites Road Wetland is accessed via Whites Road off Globe Derby Drive. The **St Kilda foreshore** is located at the sanctuary's Southern Gateway on St Kilda Bay. **Port Gawler** and the **Thompson Beach** coastline and tidal flats, are excellent natural shorebird sites. (www.tinyurl.com/adelaide-birds)

Wittunga Botanic Garden near Blackwood is a great place for spotting nectar eating birds (www.tinyurl.com/ wittunga-birds).

Gluepot Reserve, about 50 km north of Waikerie, is a birdwatchers' paradise with 190 species recorded including six that are nationally threatened (www. gluepot.org).

Kangaroo Island suffered badly in the 2019-2020 bushfires but is making

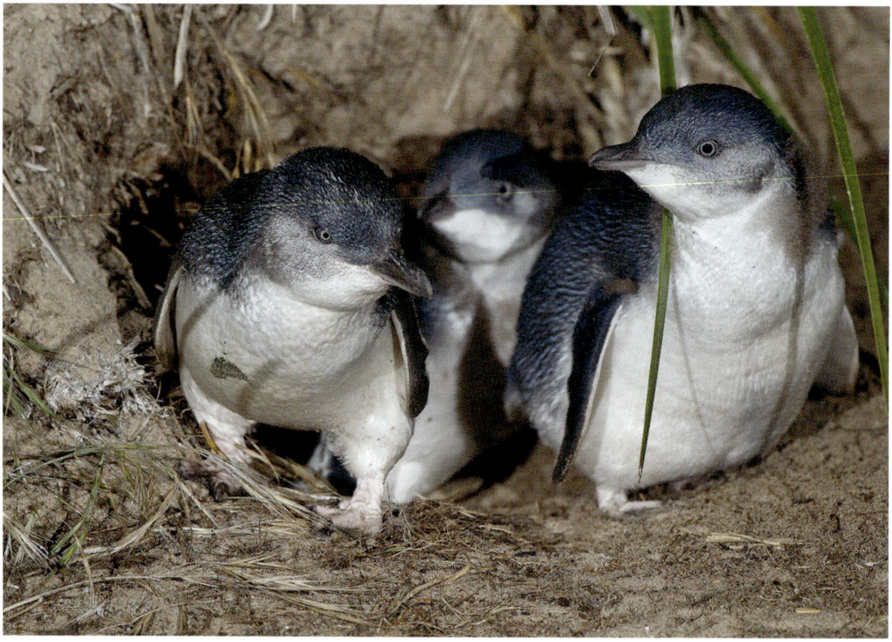

Little Penguin family exiting burrow, Bruny Island, Tasmania. © JJ Harrison. (Licensed under the Creative Commons Attribution-Share Alike 3.0 Unported license.)

a comeback. You can download a comprehensive bird-watching guide from www.tinyurl.com/ki-birds.

Birds SA provides a wealth of information for birders (www.tinyurl.com/sa-birds). There are also a number of private tour operators providing guiding services (www.tinyurl.com/sa-birds2 and www.tinyurl.com/adelaide-birds2).

Tasmania

In Hobart, **kunanyi/Mount Wellington** is a top spot for birdwatching (www.wellingtonpark.org.au). Just outside the capital, the Ramsar-listed **Pitt Water-Orielton** Lagoon is one of the only two sites in Tasmania included in the East Asian-Australasian Flyway Network (www.tinyurl.com/pwo-birds).

Near **Launceston**, the **Tamar Island Wetlands** reserve is a haven for around 60 species, which are easily spotted from the boardwalk, bird hide and picnic tables (www.tinyurl.com/tamar-birds).

Little penguins can be seen at dusk at **Penguin** east of Burnie and several other places along Tasmania's northern coast like the **Lillico Beach Conservation** Area near Devonport (www.tinyurl.com/tas-penguins).

There are also ticketed tours in Low Head, 45 minutes drive from Launceston and at the east-coast town of **Bicheno** (www.tinyurl.com/bicheno-tours).

Bruny Island is classified an Important Bird Area by BirdLife International and the **South Bruny National Park** takes you away from the more popular tourist venues (www.tinyurl.com/bruny-np).

Maria Island off the east coast is a great place to photograph sea birds dive and swoop into the ocean (www.tinyurl.com/maria-birds).

Inala Nature Tours (www.tinyurl.com/inala-birds) offer numerous Tasmanian birdwatching experiences, especially around Bruny Island. Other operators include Bellbird Birding Tours (www.bellbirdtours.com) and Shutterbug Walkabouts (www.shutterbugwalkabouts.com.au) which offers women-only Birds on Bruny photography tour.

Victoria

The **Royal Melbourne Botanic Gardens** and the banks of the Yarra River in the Warrandyte State Park provide opportunities for seeing a number of species of common regional birds (www.tinyurl.com/yarra-birds).

Other sites in the area include the **Dandenong Ranges National Park**, which attracts visitors like Latham's Snipe (summer) as well as Rails and Crakes. More sites are listed here: www.tinyurl.com/melb-birds.

Just over an hour's drive from Melbourne, **Brisbane Ranges National Park** is one of the state's richest wildflower habitats and a haven for nectar-drinking bush birds (www.tinyurl.com/bris-ranges).

Gippsland Lakes roughly 200 km from Melbourne, provides habitat for over 20,000 waterbirds some travelling from Siberia and Alaska. Good places for birding are the **Rotomah Island Bird Observatory and Jack Smith Lake State Game Reserve** (www.tinyurl.com/gippsland-birds).

Also in this region is the **Wilsons Promontory National Park**, which is good for parrots as well as a variety of bush birds (www.tinyurl.com/wilsons-birds).

Victoria's **Mallee region** provides ample opportunities for bird-watching at the **Wyperfeld National Park, Murray-Sunset National Park, Hattah-Kulkyne National Park, Kings Billabong Park** and **Little Desert National Park**. (www.tinyurl.com/vic-birds)

The **Chiltern-Mount Pilot National Park** is a great place to see and photograph birds of prey, including raptors and owls (www.tinyurl.com/chiltern-birds).

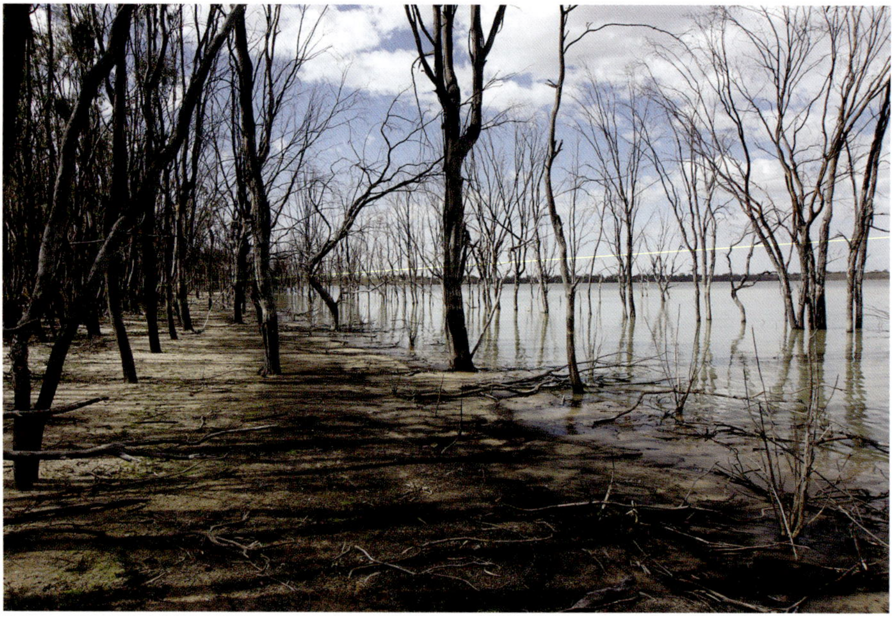

The many lakes and waterways in Victoria's Mallee region, such as Lake Mournpall in the Hattah-Kulkyne National Park shown here, provide habitats for a wide variety of inland birds. Sony ILCE-6000 camera with E PZ 16-50mm f/3.5-5.6 OSS lens at 16mm (24mm equivalent in 35mm format); ISO 100, 1/125 second at f/11; Program AE, multi-pattern metering. (Source: Camera House.)

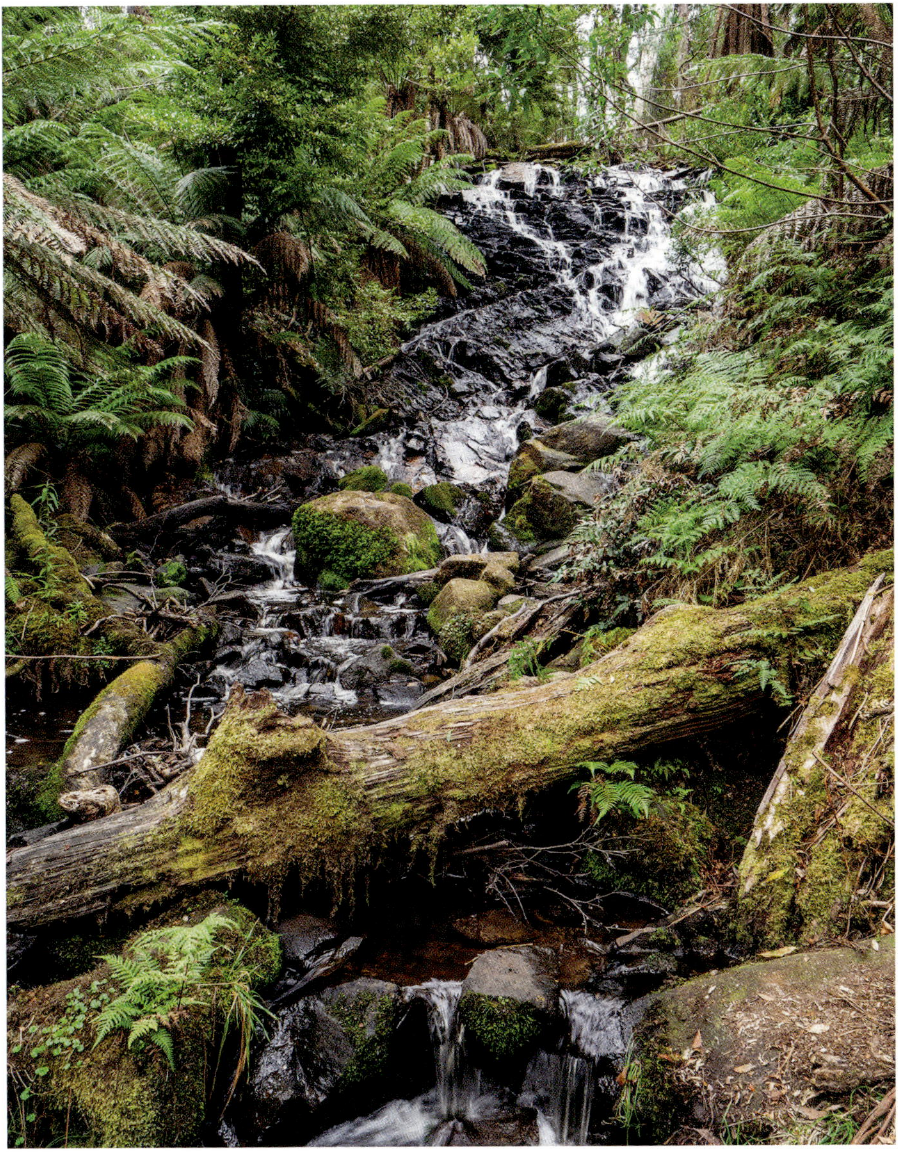

The Dandenong Ranges and Yarra Valley national and state parks provide a variety of bushland habitats within easy reach of Melbourne.

Managed by Melbourne Water and accessible by permit only, the **Western Treatment Plant (WTP)** near Werribee, 50 kms west of Melbourne, is one of Australia's most famous birding sites. In the warmer months you might see over 100 species in just one day (www.tinyurl.com/wtp-birds).

Western Australia:

Alfred Cove Nature Reserve in the Swan River estuary has more than 140 different species of birds that visit from all over the world (www.tinyurl.com/ac-birds).

Popeye Lake, one of four inner wetlands in the **Herdsman Lake Regional Park**, on the Swan Coastal Plain north-west of Perth has a floating jetty with an observation deck (www.tinyurl.com/popeye-birds). **Herdsman Lake** also contains a Discovery Centre, operated by the WA Gould League, which conducts monthly morning bird walks as well as other community-related activities (www.wagouldleague.com.au).

Also on Perth's doorstep is **Beeliar Regional Park** which protects 3400 hectares of wetland and includes 26 lakes where water birds come to nest and feed (www.tinyurl.com/brp-birds).

The **Bibra Lake Reserve** in the Beeliar Wetlands chain includes a 6 km loop walk around the lake's foreshore that has two hides overlooking the lake.

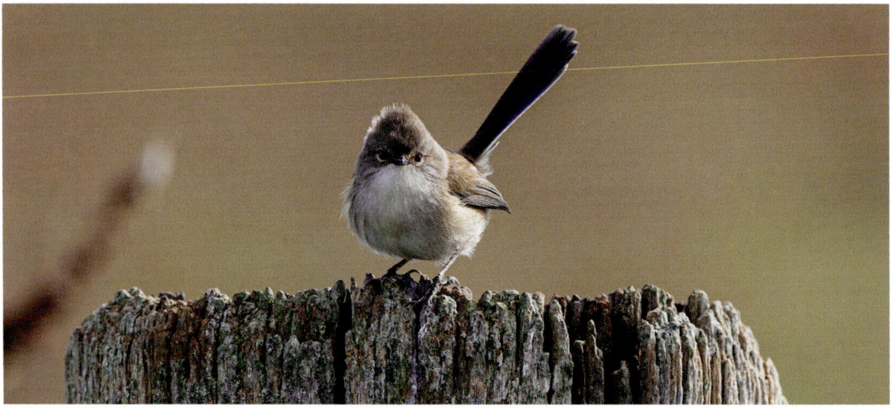

This photograph of a White-Winged Fairywren was taken at the Western Treatment Plant (WTP) near Werribee by Dani Webb of Camera House, Croydon, who describes the location as 'an incredible location for diverse birdlife'. Nikon D5 camera with AF-S NIKKOR 200-500mm f/5.6E ED VR lens at 500mm; ISO 800, 1/1250 second at f/5.6; Aperture-priority AE, multi-pattern metering. © Dani Webb.

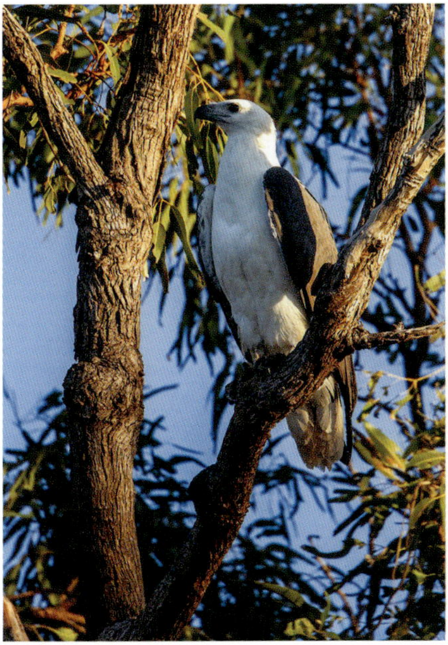

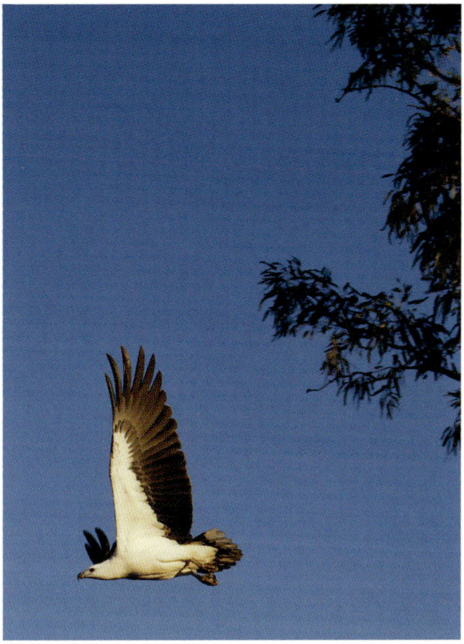

Two shots of a White-bellied Sea Eagle, taken at the Broome Bird Observatory during the winter, before the migrating shorebirds arrive. Canon EOS 5D Mark II camera with EF 70-300mm at 300mm; ISO 400, 1/500 second at f/6.7 (left); 1/750 second at f/6.7 (right); Aperture-priority AE, multi-pattern metering.

Birding is said to be good all year round and the hides are free of charge (www.tinyurl.com/blr-birds).

Broome Bird Observatory is renowned as a base for shorebird researchers and one of the best places in the world to see shorebirds year-round. It is also a good place to photograph coastal raptors (www.tinyurl.com/bbo-birds).

The **Eyre Bird Observatory**, located between the arid Nullarbor Plain to the north and the coastal waters of the Great Australian Bight to the south, is home to more than 240 species of birds – many of them rare and endangered (www.tinyurl.com/eyre-birds).

The **Bibbulmun Track** through the valleys of Kalamunda National Park in the Darling Range, 24 km to the east of Perth passes through a Jarrah-Marri forest that is home to many species of bush birds (www.tinyurl.com/mundaring-birds).

The **Lake Pollard Bird Hide** in the **Yalgorup National Park** provides views

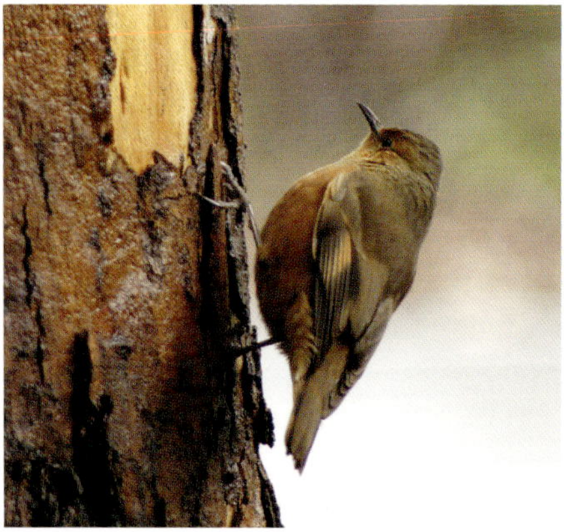

A Rufous Treecreeper photographed in the forest on the section of the Bibbulmun Track north of Walpole. Sony SLT-A55V camera with 180mm focal length, ISO1600, 1/125 second at f/5.6.

over a significant site for waterbirds that is recognised under the International Ramsar Convention (www.tinyurl.com/lake-pollard).

The **Mangrove Bay Bird Hide** in the **Cape Range National Park** on the Pilbara Coast near Exmouth has many resident birds and migratory birds flock in to feed and rest in the sheltered bay (www.tinyurl.com/mb-birds).

Parry Lagoons Nature Reserve in the Kimberley region is a Mecca for birdwatching and photography and includes a boardwalk and bird hide (www.tinyurl.com/parry-birds).

Other birdwatching sites in Western Australia can be found here: www.tinyurl.com/wa-birds.

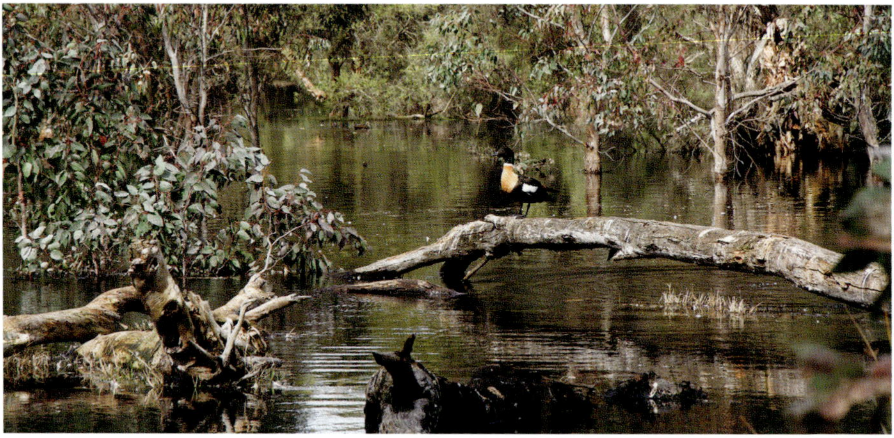

An Australian Shelduck, photographed at the Bibra Lake Reserve in the Beeliar Wetlands chain near Perth, which is reputed to be good for bird watching all year round. Nikon D90 camera with AF-S DX VR Zoom- Nikkor 18-105mm f/3.5-5.6G ED lens at 105mm; ISO 200, 1/200 second at f/10; multi-pattern metering. (Source: Camera House.)

CHAPTER 5

BIRDWATCHING HIDES

Hides (or blinds) are designed to help you to get relatively close to your subjects without startling them. They can range from a simple sheet of camouflage-patterned cloth for draping over yourself and your camera up to multi-level buildings with slot windows and shelving for resting your camera on.

Many photographers prefer camouflage clothing, plus 'skins' made from silicone or neoprene that cover their lenses and/or camera bodies. Prices range from round $50 for a lightweight hooded poncho to several hundred dollars for a full suit.

Investing in camouflage can be hit-and-miss since birds have keen eyesight and are often smart enough to detect small movements and see through disguises. Hides can conceal your movements – but only if you're very quiet.

Over time, birds become accustomed to hides so they should, in theory, provide better opportunities for getting great shots. But a lot depends on their location and how close they let you get to your quarry.

Bird hides state by state

ACT

Jerrabomberra Wetlands Nature Reserve is one of the ACT's most significant wetland habitats. Located on the Molonglo River floodplain only 4 km from Canberra's city centre it contains five bird hides that provide great views over the water and reeds (www.tinyurl.com/jw-hide).

NSW

The **Waterbird Refuge in Sydney's Bicentennial Park** should be a drawcard for bird watchers.

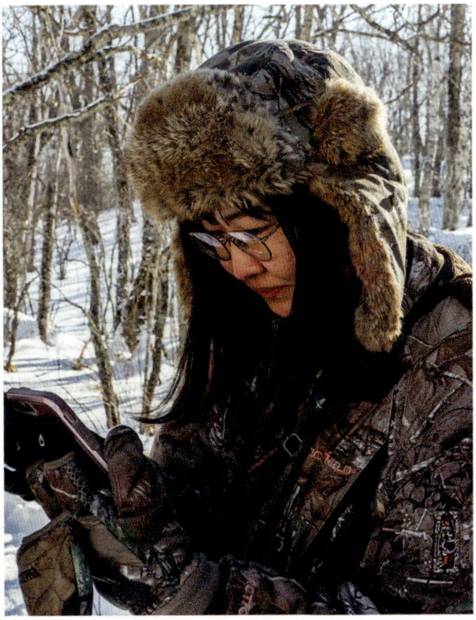

Camouflage clothing can work well in areas like forests where it blends into the background, as shown here.

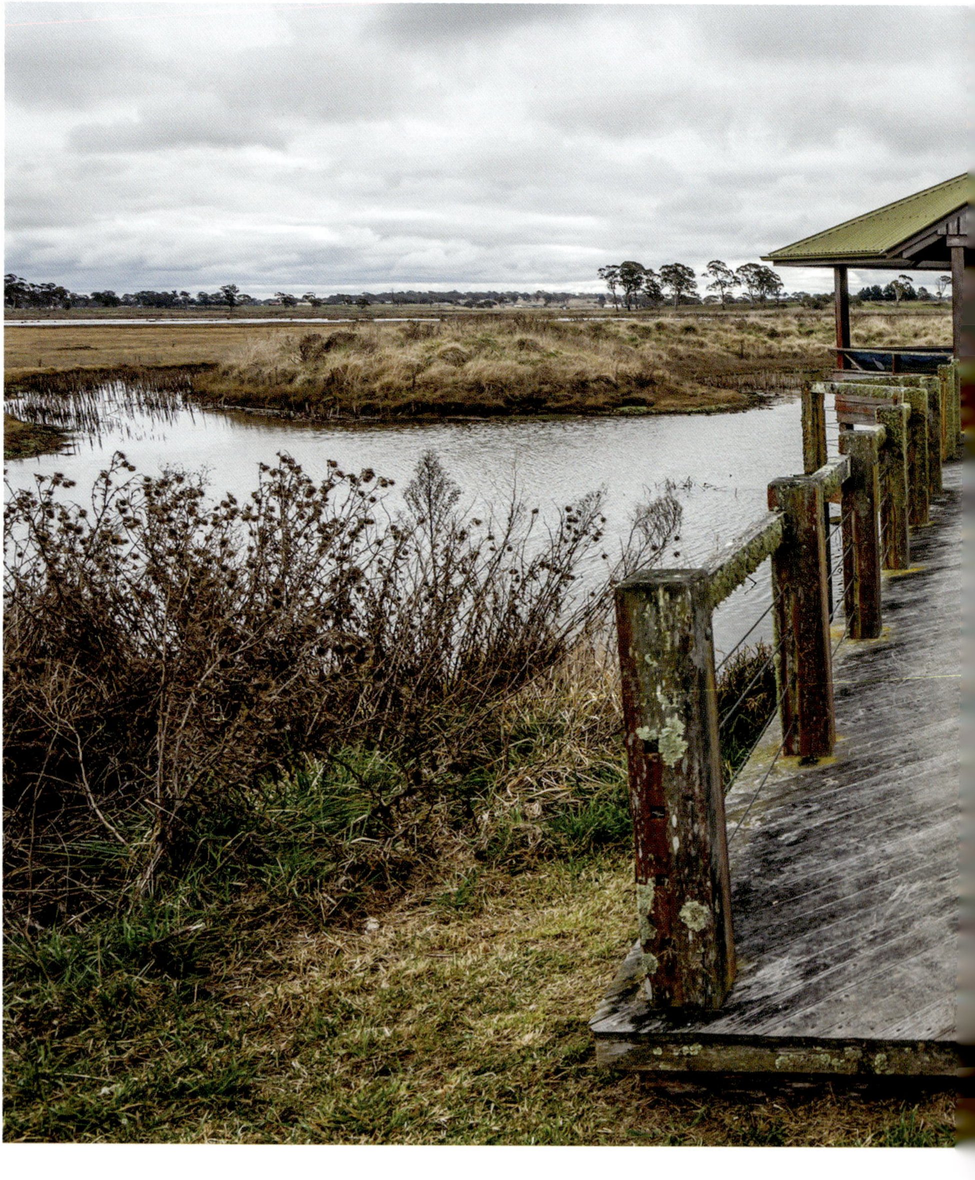

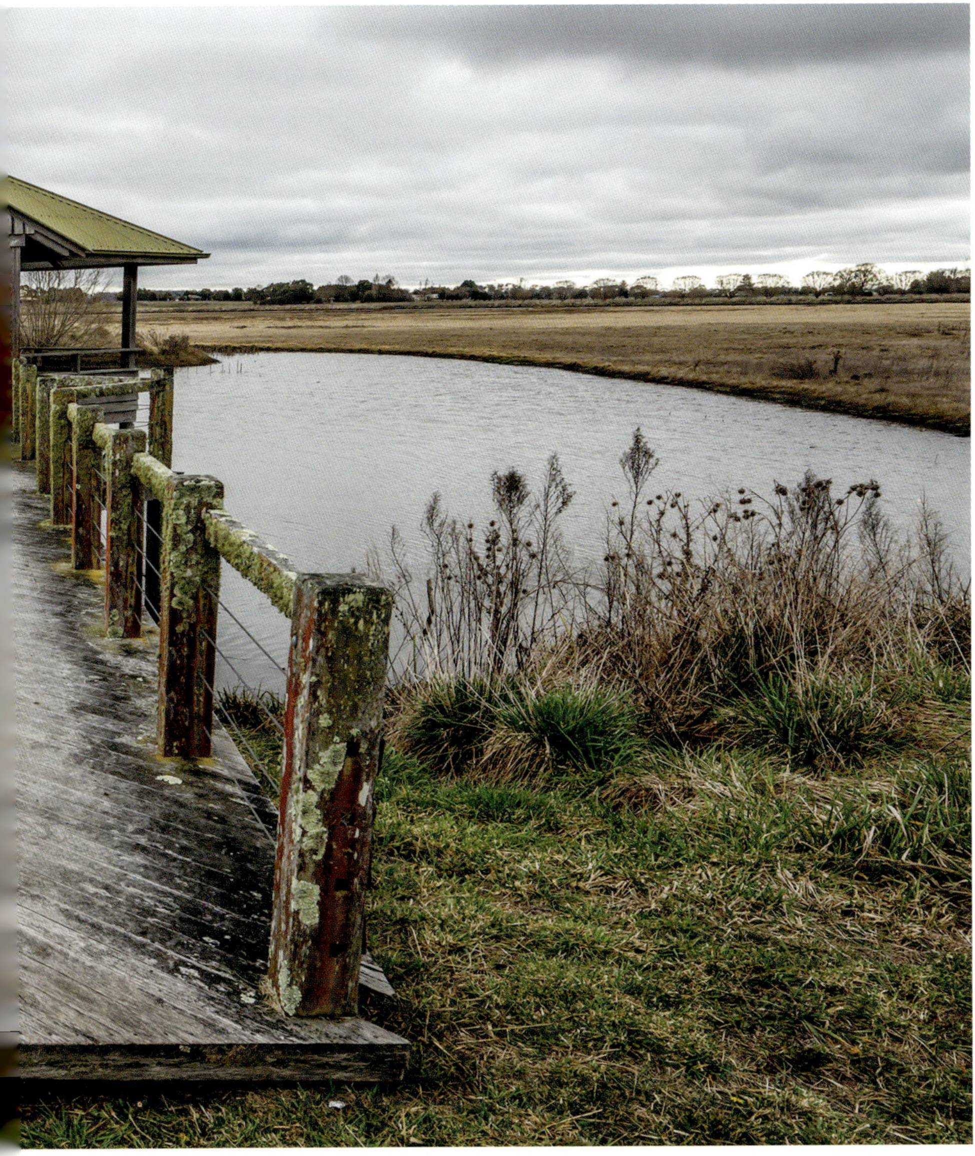

The Mother of Ducks Lagoon Nature Reserve at Guyra, 37 km north of Armidale in northern NSW. © John Spencer/DCCEEW.

Unfortunately, it's too far from the water during most of the year for lenses shorter than about 1000mm focal length. However, there are a few spots where you can photograph bush birds in the scrub alongside the access route and water birds in the shallow waterway. (www.tinyurl.com/bp-hide)

Mother of Ducks Lagoon Nature Reserve at Guyra provides a breeding place for several freshwater wetland bird species and a resting place for numerous migratory birds. Its birdwatching platform is always open and has a great view over the wetlands (www.tinyurl.com/md-hide).

There are six free of charge bird hides located around the **Wonga Wetlands near Albury**, which is home to more than 154 identified bird species. The constant wetting and drying cycle of the wetlands keeps bird numbers and diversity higher than a natural system (www.tinyurl.com/ww-hide).

Cattai Wetlands near Coopernook has a 4 km circular walk around the central wetlands which are among the most reliable places for seeing the endangered Black-necked Stork and many other species of forest and wetlands birds (www.tinyurl.com/cattai-hide).

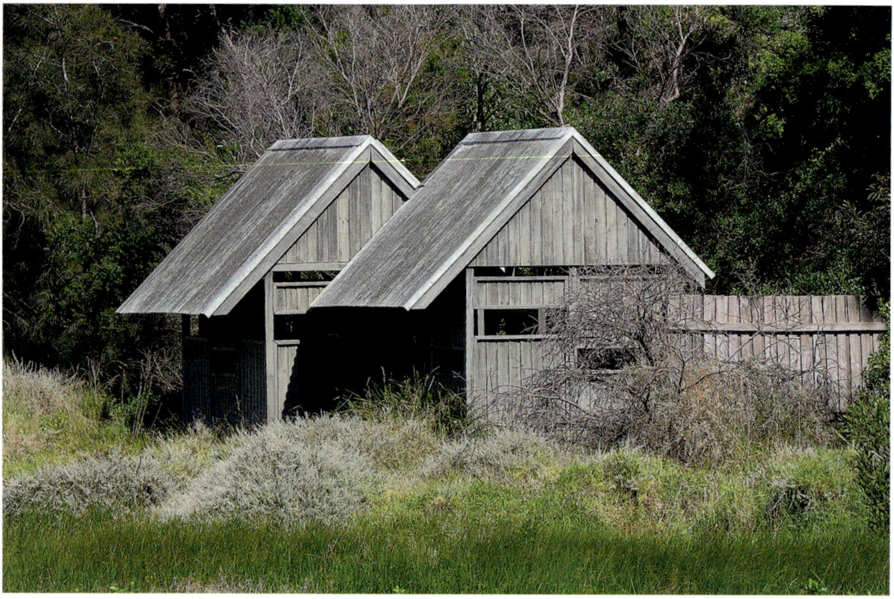

The bird-watching hide in the Waterbird Refuge at Bicentennial Park is beautifully designed but you'll need a very long telephoto lens to get close-ups of birds.

Best behaviour

When you're in a hide follow these simple guidelines:

1. Be prepared. Have your camera set up ready to go with the shutter set on silent mode before entering the hide.

2. Be patient. Wait for the birds to come to you. Most birds – particularly bush birds - are inquisitive. If you sit still and wait they'll often come close to check you out.

3. Be quiet. Don't talk and wriggle about. Avoid nylon jackets that rustle, shoes that squeak and noisy zippers – and also clothing that reflects UV light. Birds have exceptional hearing and can detect UV light.

4. Be at the right place at the right time. Birds are generally most active at the beginning and end of the day and often hide around noon.

5. Be informed about where the birds you want to photograph are; if possible having an exact location.

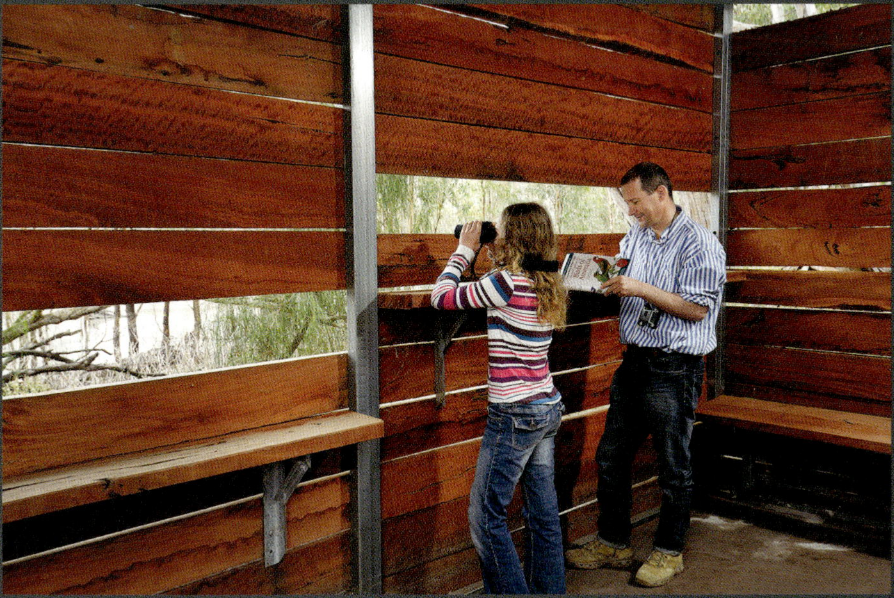

Inside the bird hide located in the Yanga Lake area Yanga National Park (also known as Murrumbidgee Valley National Park). The hide is a great spot to watch Pelicans and Black Swans as they forage for food and rear their young. © Gavin Hansford/DCCEEW

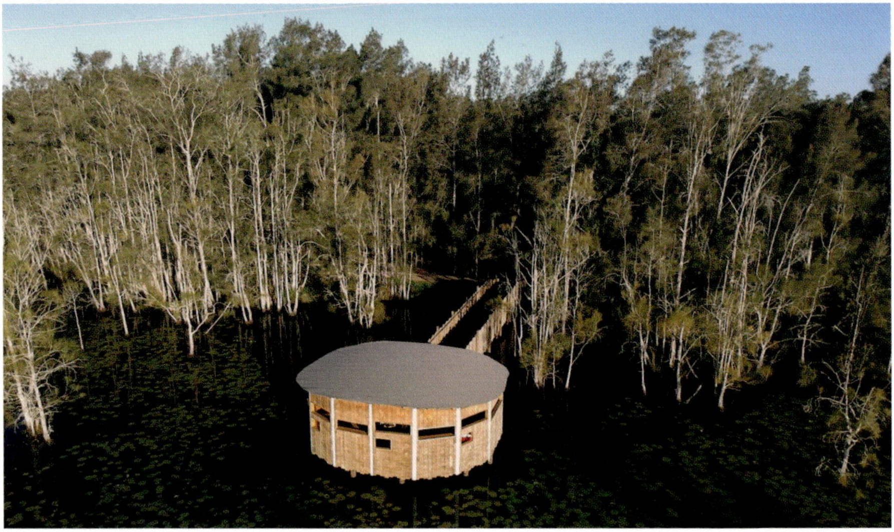

One of the two bird hides overlooking the Cattai Wetlands which provide excellent opportunities to photograph water birds. (Source: MidCoast Council.)

Gum Swamp near Forbes is a popular location for both the birdlife and birders, with four hides overlooking the water (www.tinyurl.com/gs-hide).

The **Hunter Wetlands Centre near Newcastle** has four purpose-built hides including one over the water at Water Ribbon Swamp, plus the Egret Tower overlooking Melaleuca Swamp (www.tinyurl.com/gum-swamp).

The **Gwydir Wetlands State Conservation Area** is one of the few preserved inland wetlands remaining in the Murray-Darling Basin. Its semi-permanent waterholes attract a wide variety of water birds when they fill with water. (www.tinyurl.com/wl-hide)

Part of **Lake Cargelligo** in western NSW has been designated a bird sanctuary – with two accessible bird hides. Binoculars and bird guides can be hired from the Lake Cargelligo tourist information centre (at the lake end of the main street). (www.tinyurl.com/lakec-hide)

Yanga Lake in the Murray-Riverina region near Balranald protects vital feeding and breeding grounds for more than 150 species of migratory and water birds. It has a viewing deck with pedestal binoculars for close up views of spoonbills, herons and glossy ibis (www.tinyurl.com/yl-hide).

Boyters Lane Bird Hide at Jerseyville on the way into South West Rocks is located in a tranquil area of

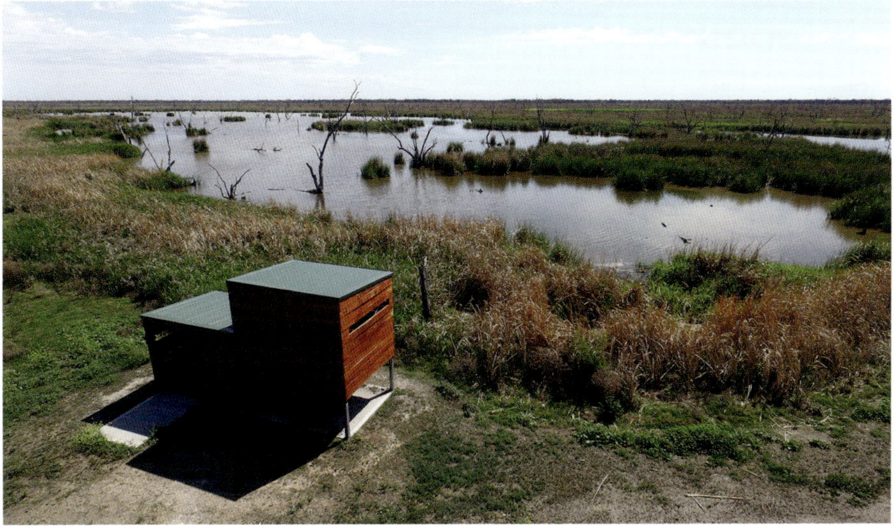

Aerial view of the Waterbird Lagoon bird hide in the Gwydir Wetlands State Conservation Area. © James Faris/DCCEEW.

rehabilitated bushland, mangrove and salt marsh (www.tinyurl.com/bl-hide).

NT

Fogg Dam Conservation Reserve, a 45-minute drive from Darwin, includes a number of shaded viewing areas and hides along the dam wall (www.tinyurl.com/fd-hide).

Mamukala wetlands in the **Kakadu National Park** has a number of bird hides and viewing shelters (www.tinyurl.com/mw-hide).

Queensland

The Sunshine Coast City Council has installed a bird hide at **Park Lakes, Bli Bli** (www.tinyurl.com/pl-hide).

The Burdekin Shire Council in North Queensland has constructed a bird hide in the edge of **Horseshoe Lagoon**, about 30 minutes by car from Ayr on the Bruce Highway (www.tinyurl.com/hl-hide).

Coalstoun Lakes National Park near Bundaberg has two bird hides along the 4.4 km track, with the first bird hide at 800 metres from the start and the second bird hide at the 2.2 km point (www.tinyurl.com/clnp-hide).

Tyto wetlands near Ingham has several viewing platforms and bird hides, including a dawn/dusk viewing platform for spotting Grass Owls and a well designed main hide (www.tinyurl.com/tw-hide).

Situated between the Daintree Rainforest and the Great Barrier Reef, **Thala Beach Lodge** in Port Douglas attracts an array of bird life. The **Osprey Bird Hide** on the forest edge and overlooking the Macalister Range provides visitors a rare opportunity of watching Osprey feed their young in a natural habitat (www.tinyurl.com/osprey-hide).

Hasties Swamp on the Atherton Tablelands, just 4 km from Atherton town centre is overlooked by a two-storey hide that allows photographers to capture shots of water birds and at least seven raptor species (www.tinyurl.com/hs-hide).

The **Townsville Town Common** is home to approximately 280 bird species. The Freshwater trail passes two bird hides, which are close to the Freshwater car park (www.tinyurl.com/ttc-hide).

SA

There are 5 bird hides at **Gluepot Reserve**, 50 km from Waikerie, each named after people who have made a major contribution to the reserve (www.tinyurl.com/gp-hide). Gluepot is part of the largest block of intact mallee left in Australia and home to six nationally threatened bird species plus a further 17 regionally threatened bird species. Day Entry and

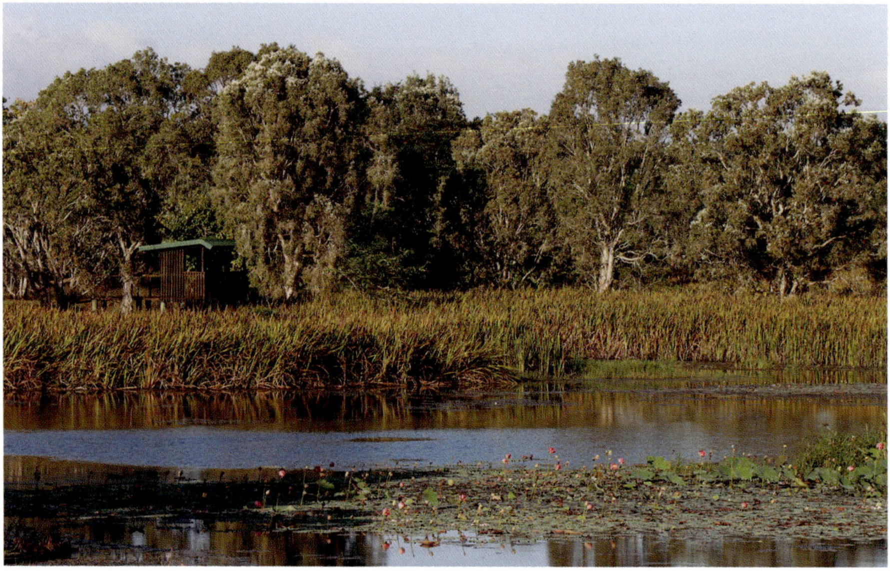

A view of one of the bird hides in the Tyto wetlands near Ingham, showing its proximity to both bush and water. © Malcolm Tattersall; www.malcolmtattersall.com.au

Camping can be booked and paid for online at www.tinyurl.com/gp-book.

Big Swamp on the Flinders Highway, 20 km NE of Port Lincoln has a bird hide which overlooks the central basin in a small area accessible to the public off the Flinders Highway where it crosses a causeway between the central and northern basins (www.tinyurl.com/big-swamp).

The **Fox Lake Bird Hide near the Robe Holiday Park** provides views of wetland birds, including the migratory Latham's Snipe and Red-necked Stint (www.tinyurl.com/fl-hide).

Hart Lagoon near Waikerie in the South Australian Riverland has a bird hide at the south-eastern end of the lagoon (www.tinyurl.com/hart-hide).

Tasmania

The **Tamar Island Wetlands Centre on the outskirts of Launceston** has a bird hide about 500 metres from the start of the boardwalk where visitors can see several species of duck, black swans, egrets, cormorants and swamp harriers (www.tinyurl.com/ti-hide).

Inala Nature Reserve on Bruny Island has a Raptor Photography Hide that is purpose-designed for bird

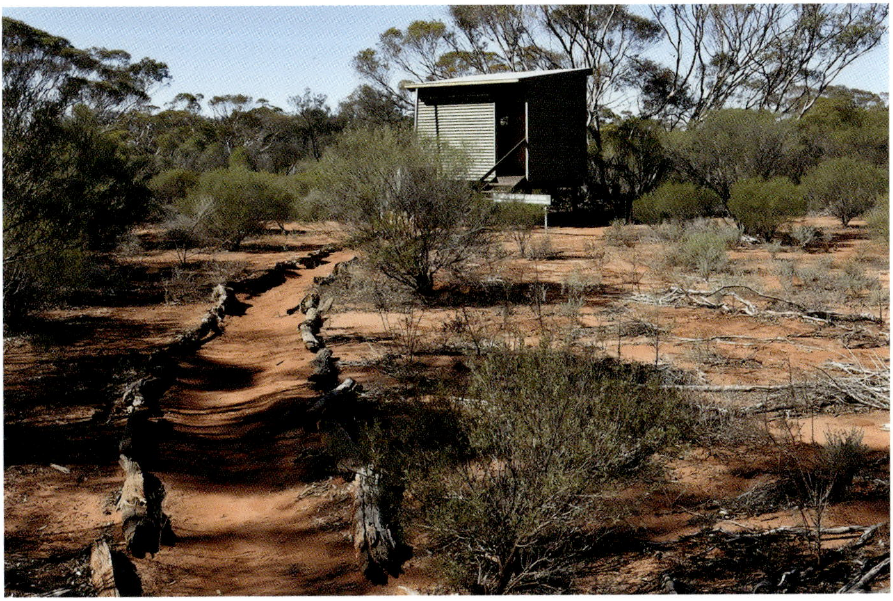

The Don and Chris Hill bird hide at Gluepot Reserve. © Stephen Langman.

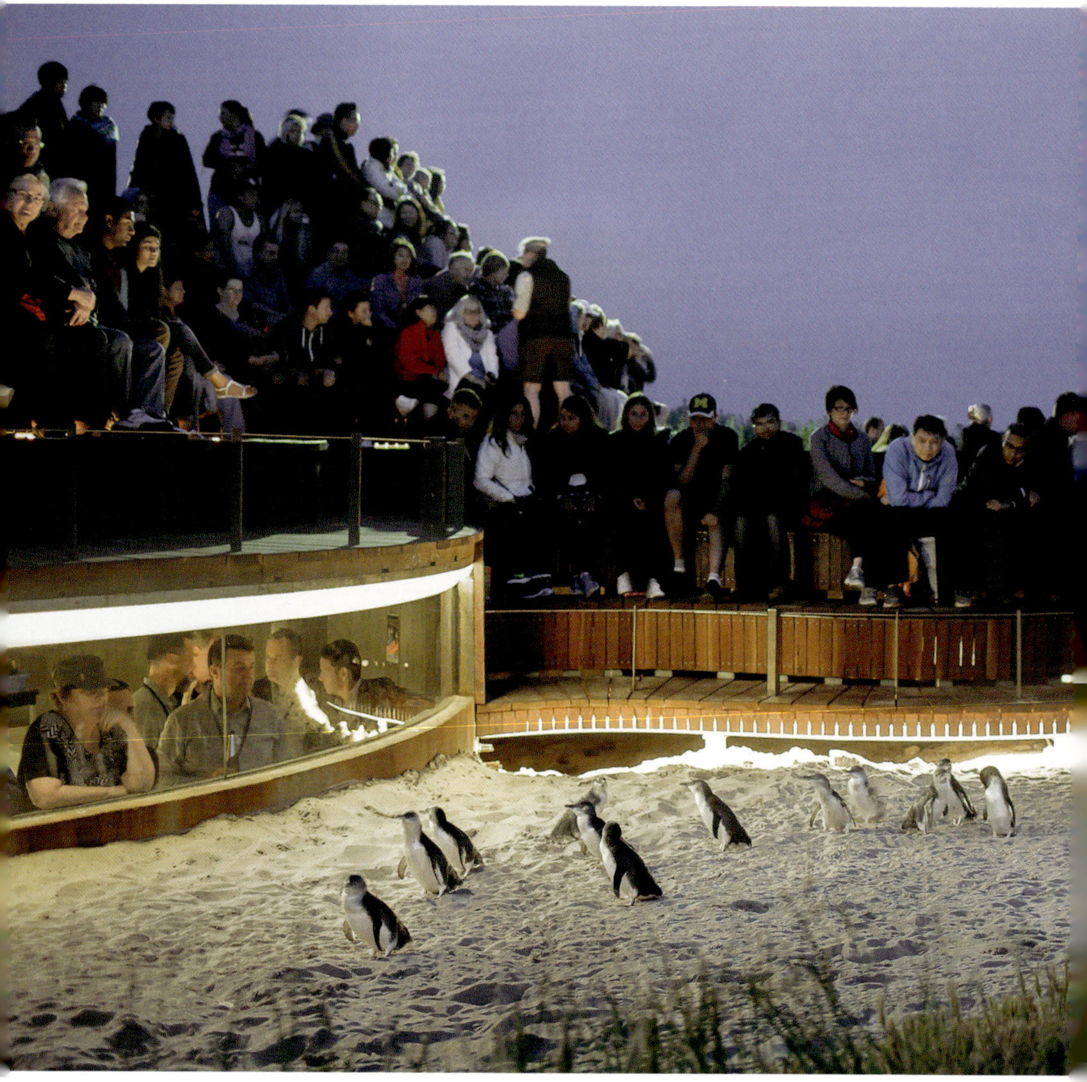

Visitors to Phillip Island's Penguin Parade have plenty of opportunities to obtain close-up shots of the famous Little Penguins returning to their burrows at dusk. © Phillip Island Nature Parks.

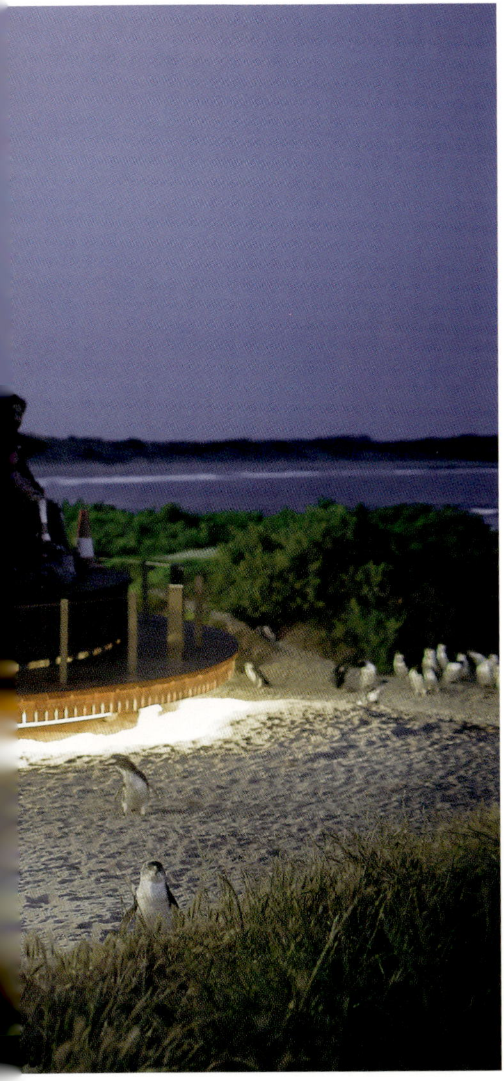

photographers (www.tinyurl.com/inala-hide). Three cottages on the site are open for bookings and on-site guests can use the hide at discounted prices.

Victoria

Serendip Sanctuary 60 kms west of Melbourne has a number of bird hides where visitors can see some of the 150 bird species that breed in and visit the sanctuary (www.tinyurl.com/ss-hide).

Phillip Island off the Bass Coast is renowned for its nightly Penguin Parade but also includes a Twitcher Trail with two bird hides that provide good views of a range of water birds. Fisher's Wetland, also in this area, has boardwalks with bird hides and elevated platforms, while there is another bird hide at Baxter's Wetland. (www.tinyurl.com/pi-hide)

There are two hides in the **South Gippsland** region of Victoria: one at **Bald Hills Wetland Reserve** and the other, a Ramsar Site, is **Toora Bird Hide** nestled at the crown of Corner Inlet. Central Gippsland has the **Rotomah Island Bird Observatory**. (www.tinyurl.com/sg-hide)

More than 200 different bird species have been spotted in **Point Cook Coastal Park** and neighbouring **Cheetham Wetlands near Melbourne**, where birds travel from places as far away as Siberia. Bird hides are provided in Point Cook Coastal Park (www.tinyurl.com/vic-hides) and at Spectacle Lake (www.tinyurl.com/sl-hide).

Explore the Mallee (www.tinyurl.com/mallee-hides) is a local eco-tourism business run by Louise Nicholas and Michael Gooch. Based in **Patchewollock**, the site has two bird hides located at permanent water points, each accommodating two people. A guided tour must be completed prior to booking the bird hides to allow the owners to point out bird hot spots and explain access and restricted areas.

The **Reed Beds Bird Hide boardwalk at Mathoura** in the Murray Valley National Park has an impressive, two-storey hide overlooking the wetlands (www.tinyurl.com/rb-hide).

Nhill Swamp Wildlife Reserve in North-Western Victoria includes a short trail through woodland that includes a bird hide (www.tinyurl.com/ns-hide).

WA

There are two bird hides – Baumea and Balgay – on the northern edge of **Herdsman Lake** approximately 7 km northwest of Perth City, reachable by a track off Jon Sanders Drive (www.tinyurl.com/baumea-hide).

Albany on the South Coast of **Western Australia** is close to several wetlands areas with a varied range of

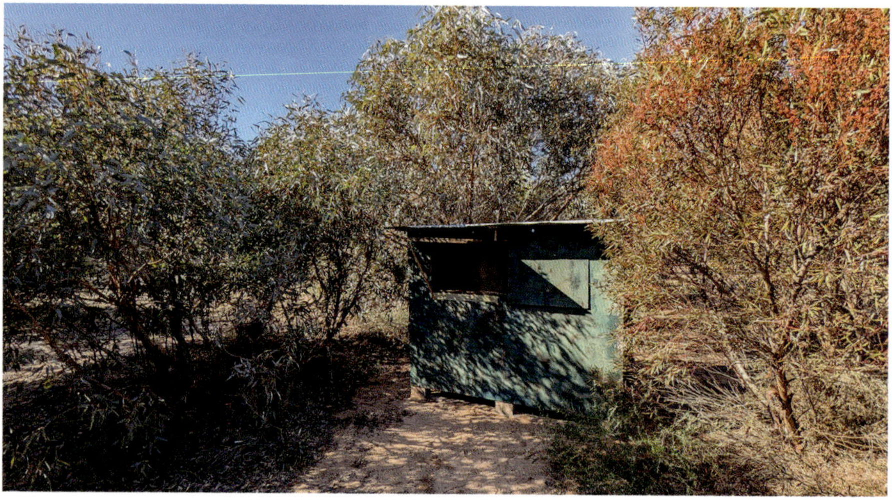

One of the two bird hides at Explore the Mallee near Patchewollock in north-western Victoria. (Image supplied by Explore the Mallee.)

bird species. The Lake Seppings Bird Walk offers hides and easy access (www.tinyurl.com/lsbird-hide).

The **Lake Pollard Bird Hide in the Yalgorup National Park** overlooks a significant wetland that is recognised under the International Ramsar Convention (www.tinyurl.com/lpbird-hide).

Dongara on the Brand Highway south of Geraldton has a 4.6 km loop trail that includes river margins, samphire wetland, a bird hide near the river mouth and boardwalks to access the estuary (www.tinyurl.com/dongara-hide).

The **Wulyibidi Yanayina walking trail at Monkey Mia** has a bird hide where you may be able to spot Common Bronzewing, Crested Pigeon, Zebra Finch and Emu (www.tinyurl.com/wy-hide).

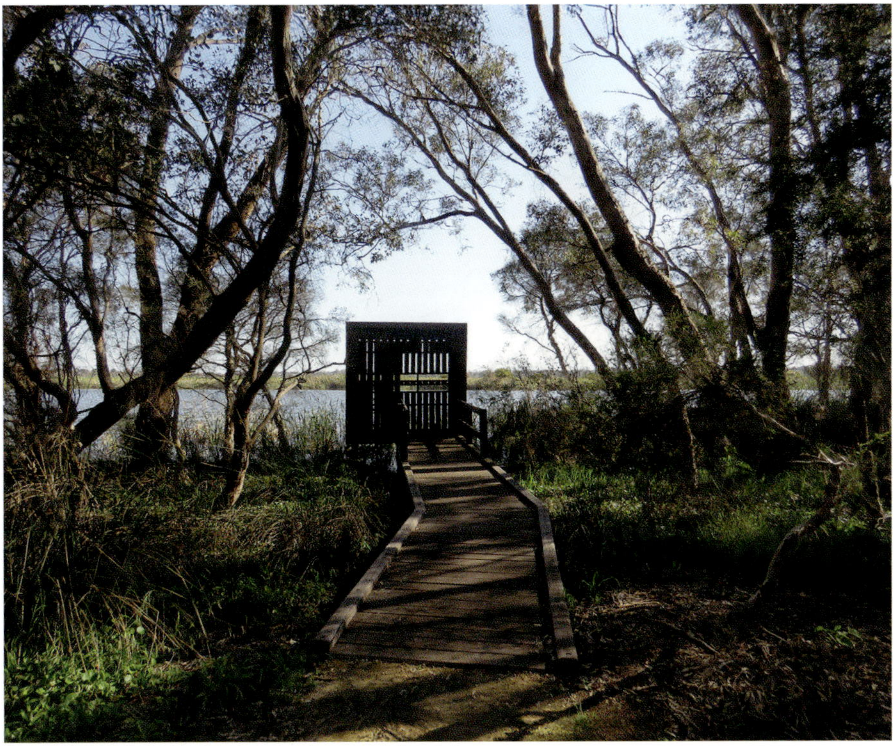

The Baumea bird hide at Herdsman Lake near Perth. © Calistemon. Used under the Creative Commons Attribution-Share Alike 4.0 International license.

CHAPTER 6

SHOOTING TIPS

Before embarking on a shoot, try to have your camera set up and ready to use, regardless of whether you're working from a hide or in the field. This means choosing the file format, setting sensitivity limits and deciding on exposure controls. In this chapter we outline the main functions to address.

File format

Record raw files wherever you can because they give you more image data to work with. In contrast to JPEGs, raw files capture as much image data as possible. JPEGs are much smaller files – but the JPEG compression process discards important data you could use.

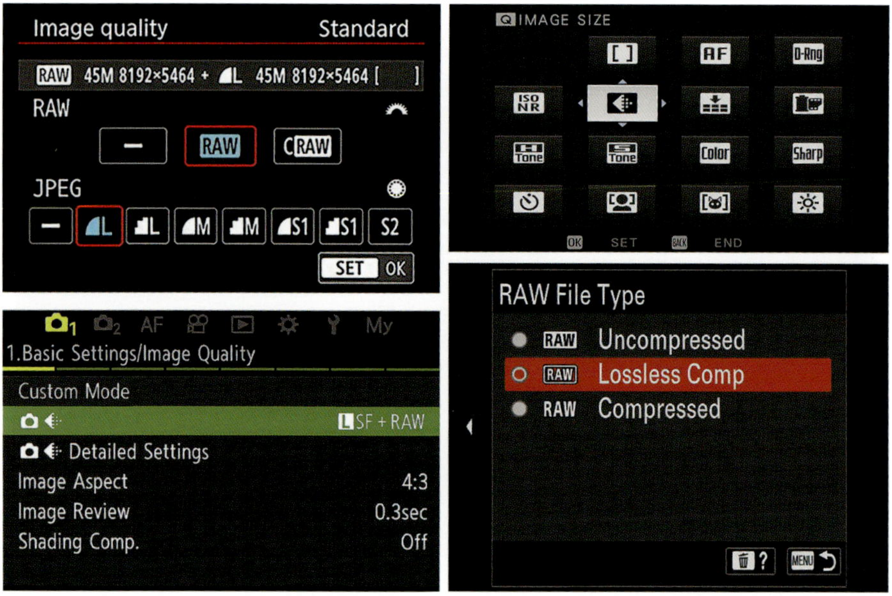

Some typical menu pages for setting file formats from different camera manufacturers, clockwise from top left: Canon EOS R, Fujifilm Quick Menu, Sony raw file compression options, OM systems RAW+JPEG selection.

If you want both file formats, select RAW+JPEG and save space by selecting smaller JPEG file sizes.

Many cameras provide several raw file settings, typically uncompressed, compressed and losslessly compressed. Compressing files discards some information to make the file smaller but retains critical data. Losslessly compressed raw files are slightly larger but preserve ALL the image data.

However, uncompressed files can be very large. Choose this setting only if you have plenty of storage space in your camera.

Shooting mode

Many bird photographers prefer using the Aperture Priority (A or Av) mode so they can set a wide aperture, ideally no smaller than f/5.6. Most lenses perform best at wide apertures and you need as

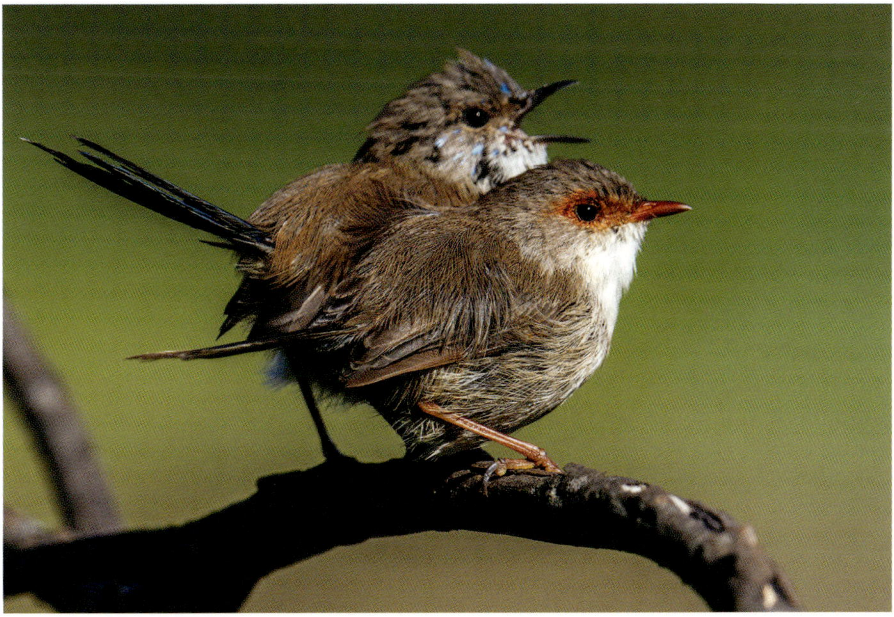

Recent cameras, like the OM-1 Mark II used for this shot paired with the sophisticated M.Zuiko Digital ED 150-600mm f/5.0-6.3 IS lens come with powerful image stabilisation and provide enough magnification for close-up shots of tiny fledgling Fairy Wrens. A hand-held shot at ISO 200, 500mm focal length (equivalent to 1000mm in 35mm format), 1/500 second at f/6.3.

much light as possible to support fast shutter speeds, particularly when using longer telephoto lenses.

When shooting birds in flight, boost ISO sensitivity and stop down to around f/8 for enough depth of field to record the entire bird sharply. Make sure your shutter speed is fast enough to prevent motion blurring or pan the camera to follow the subject's motion. Consider capturing a burst of shots.

Shutter settings

If your camera has a silent shutter mode, we'd recommend using it as birds have excellent hearing and the click of the shutter can startle them. You'll also need shutter speeds of at least 1/500 second to capture a bird that's in motion.

Slower shutter speeds are fine for perched birds or birds on the ground and when panning or if you want to blur the bird's wing-beats to suggest rapid movement. If your camera and/or lens are stabilised you may be able to reduce shutter speeds even further.

ISO settings

Set your camera to Auto ISO and use the menu to limit the range of sensitivities the camera can use. The camera will select the lowest ISO possible under the prevailing conditions to optimise image quality.

We recommend an upper limit of ISO 3200 for most mid-to-high-end cameras, although many 'full frame' models produce relatively noise-free images at higher ISO settings. Some cameras let you set a minimum shutter speed in Auto ISO mode.

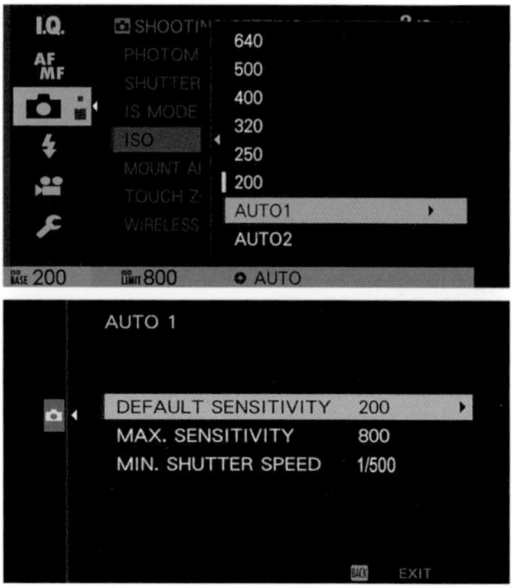

Two pages from a Fujifilm camera's menu showing how you can set the limits for the Auto ISO control to increase the likelihood of obtaining sharp images.

Optimal settings vary, depending on whether you want to print your photos or view them online. Test your camera beforehand to find out how high you can go for each scenario.

AF and metering modes

Single (or one-shot) AF is best for shooting stills, while continuous AF is best when recording a burst of shots – or video clips.

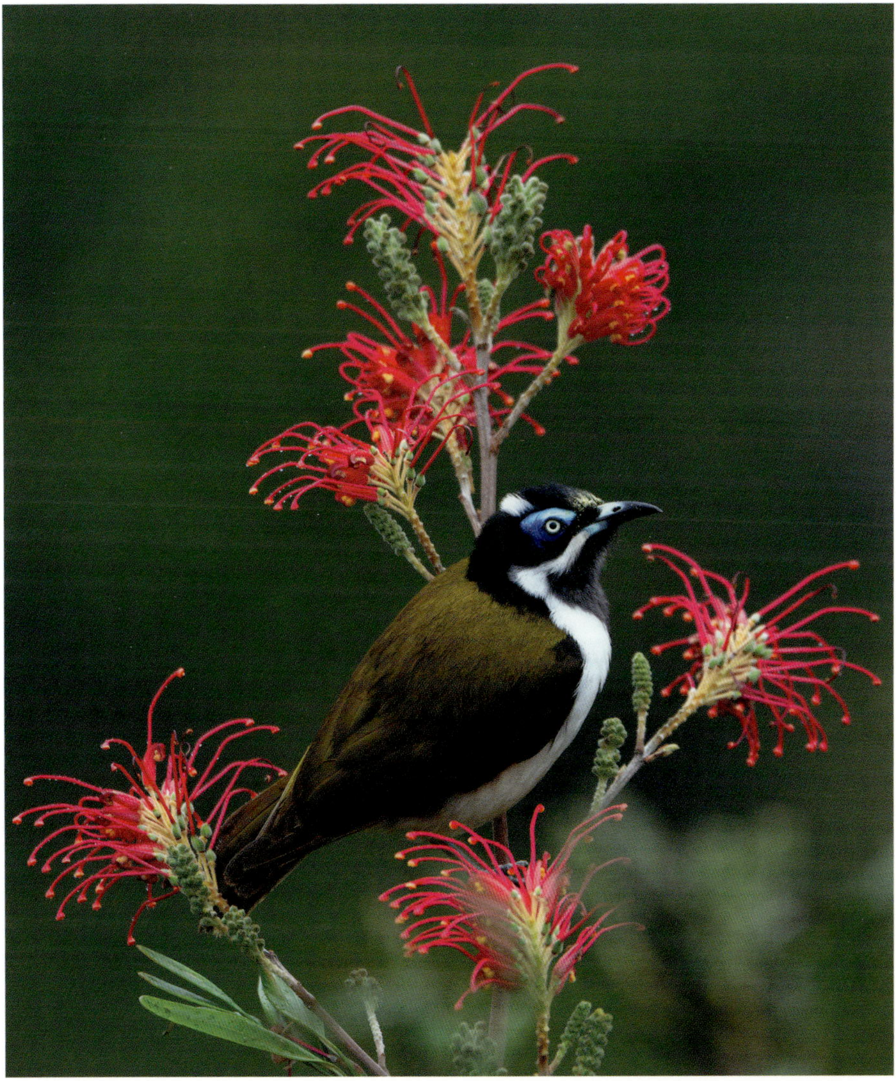

This portrait of a Blue-faced Honeyeater was taken near Modanville in northern NSW by Lachlan Cooper of Camera House Lismore using a Nikon D850 camera with a Sigma 150-600mm f/5-6.3 Sport lens at 600mm. ISO 1000, 1/100 second at f/6.3. © Lachlan Cooper.

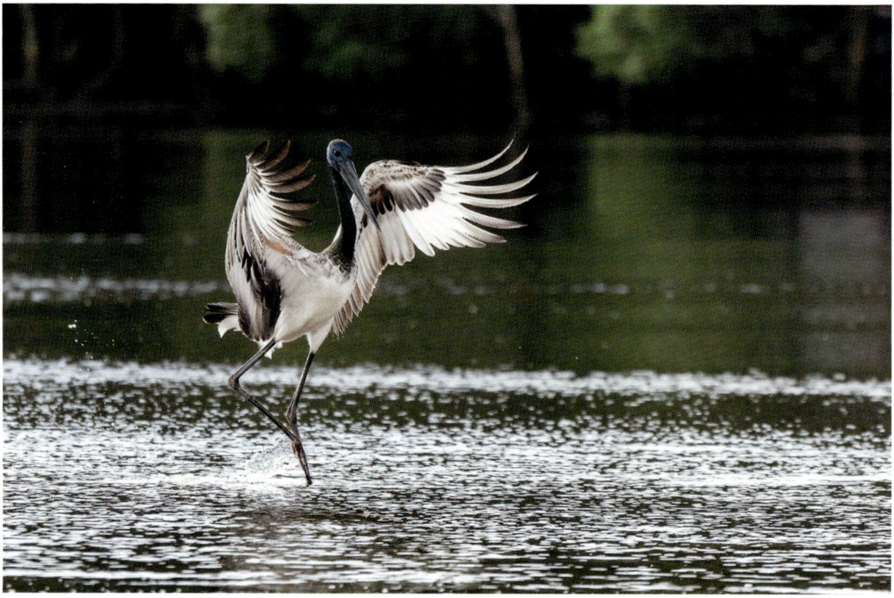

Spot metering was used for this great action shot of a Black-necked Stork, taken near Ballina by Lachlan Cooper of Camera House Lismore. Nikon D850 camera with Sigma 150-600mm f/5-6.3 Sport lens at 600mm; ISO 3200, 1/500 second at f/7.1. © Lachlan Cooper.

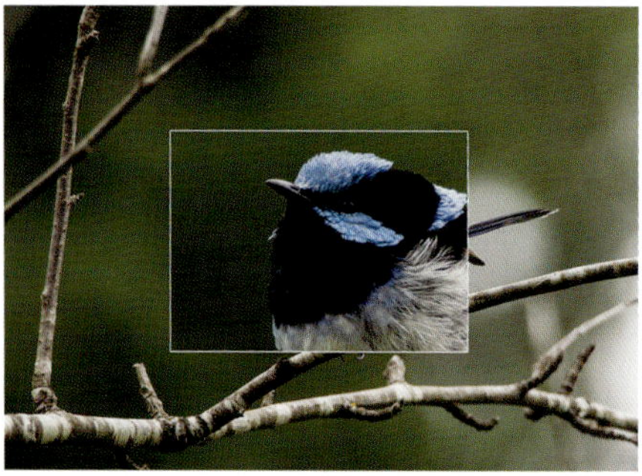

In most cameras manual focus over-ride will automatically magnify part of the image, usually around the focus point.

AF Point Selection should be set to centre or full-area and metering should be set to centre-weighted average. (If you use a Canon camera, Partial is another option.) Use Spot metering when subjects are backlit or in contrasty lighting

AF Point Expansion (Canon cameras) or Dynamic AF-Area Mode (Nikon cameras) can be used to increase the focus area when tracking moving targets. If your camera includes Subject-detection AF, use bird detection, if it's provided;

otherwise animal detection should provide some advantage. Eye detection should be engaged wherever possible.

When you need to fine-tune the focus using manual adjustments, use the default magnification preview (shown in the illustration on the adjacent page) to focus on the precise area you want. Lenses that support manual focus override or provide a pull-back manual focus 'clutch' let you switch quickly between auto and manual focus.

Spot metering makes it easier to record subject detail in backlit situations. Some cameras let you expand the metered area while Canon cameras provide a 'Partial' metering mode that takes in more of the subject.

When further adjustment is needed, use the exposure compensation (+/- icon) control. The + setting increases brightness, while the – settings reduces it. Most cameras adjust exposure in 1/3EV steps.

Drive modes

Some photographers prefer using continuous (burst) drive modes to improve their chances of getting at least one sharp shot. Unfortunately, it's not totally fail-safe and you can end up with hundreds of images filling your memory card.

Many newer cameras include pre-capture modes that are more effective and less memory-hungry. They work by starting to record frames when you half-press the shutter button (which also focuses the lens) and continuing until you release the button. Look for settings like Pre-Shot, Pro-Capture or Pre-Release. Olympus (now OM System) cameras were the first to introduce this feature and still offer the most configurable settings.

Some cameras limit recording times but most let you select the maximum frame rate plus the number of frames to record before and after the shutter is fully pressed. These settings can be stored in the camera's Custom Modes, where you can set different parameters for different situations. When used with bird detection AF, they can yield a high percentage of sharp frames.

Video

Every camera – and most smartphones – can record video at a minimum resolution of 4K (3840 x 2160 pixels). Some can capture even larger frames (6K or 8K in high-end cameras). Many photographers don't realise they can extract still frames from a video clip as JPEGs.

A 4K frame has a resolution of just over eight megapixels, which is high enough to print at A3 size. Note that video frames are usually recorded with a 16:9 aspect ratio, although some cameras provide other aspect ratios you can choose from.

All video cameras support frame rates of at least 24 frames/second (fps), even at maximum resolution. Many go as high as 60 fps for 4K or slightly larger frame sizes.

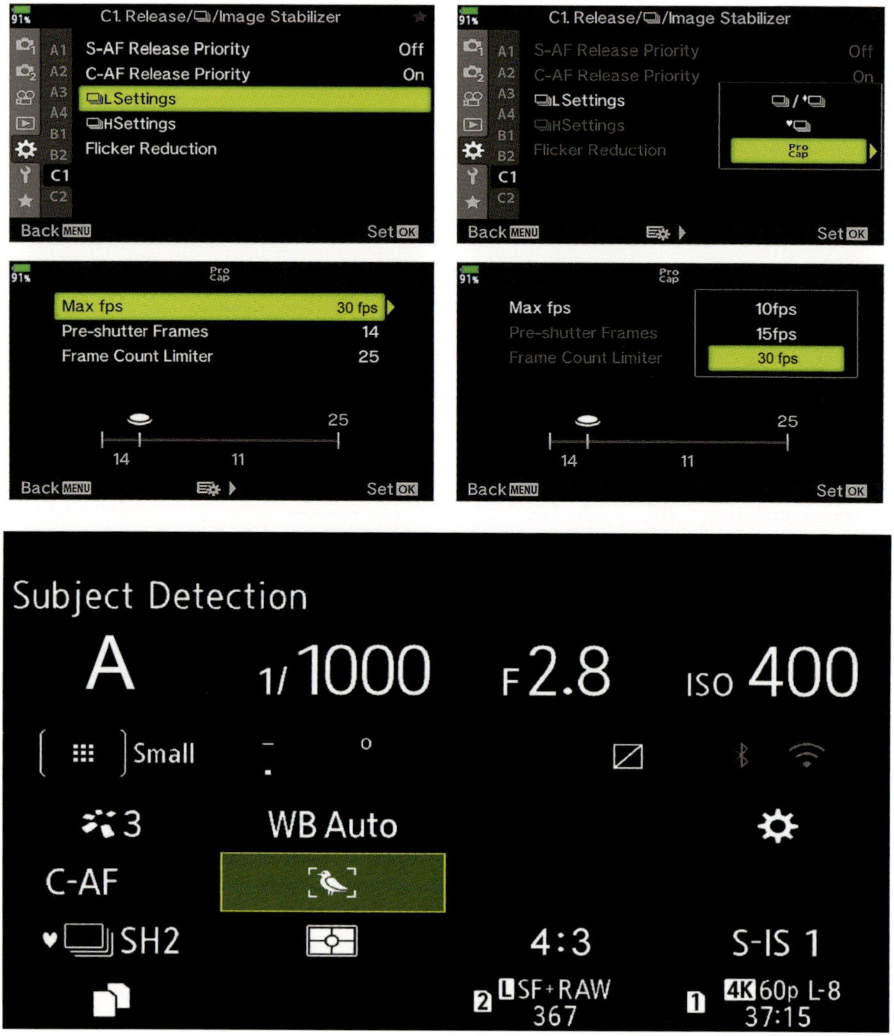

The Pro-Capture mode in the latest OM System cameras, shown in the upper section of this illustration, lets you set the frame rate and number of frames to record before and after the shutter button is pressed. Good results are possible when it's combined with bird detection, shown in the lower area.

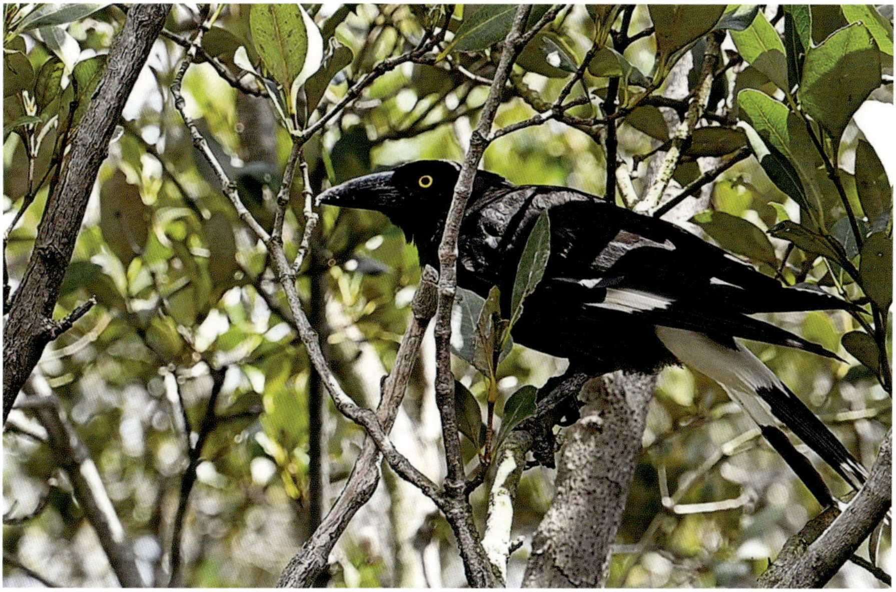

This image was recorded as a frame in a 4K video clip, showing the potential for obtaining printable photos when video is all you've recorded.

A frame from a 6K video clip has a resolution of approximately 20.5 megapixels, while an 8K frame (7680 x 4320 pixels) is just over 33 megapixels. This can make it worth shooting video when photographing rapid action, knowing you can make good quality prints from individual frames.

Handheld photography guidelines

Before in-built image stabilisation (IBIS), a simple rule of thumb for shooting handheld required the shutter speed to be equal to (or faster than) the reciprocal of the lens focal length. In other words, if you were using a 200mm lens, the slowest shutter speed should be 1/200 second.

Since the introduction of IBIS, many cameras (and some lenses) are claiming six to eight stops of exposure compensation. Such claims should always be tested. While one photographer may be able to achieve the claimed compensation four shots out of five, another may struggle to manage one out of five.

Consider the weight of your equipment. Lightweight equipment may be hard to keep steady, but a camera and lens weighing more than 2.5 kilograms is much more difficult to steady when shooting hand-held.

To improve your chances of obtaining sharp shots for hand-held shooting, try the following:

1. Increase the ISO value so you can increase shutter speeds. Most cameras perform well at ISO 1600 or higher – and many produce relatively noise-free images at ISO 6400 – or higher. Most image editors and raw file converters provide noise-reduction processing.

2. Keep your camera as still as possible. If you're in a hide, rest your camera on a ledge; in a vehicle, use the back of a seat or a rolled-down window. Lean against a post or wall – or even a tree. Sit down with your knees raised and prop the lens on them.

3. Small beanbags can also be used. They're easy to make and can be filled with dried beans or grains of rice.

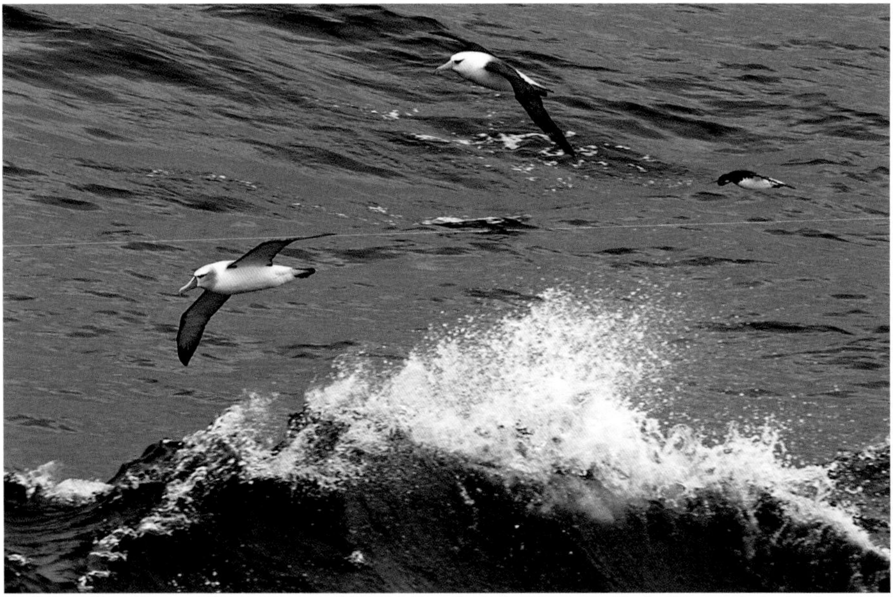

This photo of two Black-browed Albatross and an Antarctic Petrel 'surfing' a wave was captured from a ship using a cropped-sensor DSLR camera with an 480mm equivalent lens focal length using ISO 400 with a shutter speed of 1/800 second at f/10. Canon EOS 400D camera with EF 70-300mm f/4-5.6 IS USM lens at 300mm.

Backgrounds

Check your surroundings on arrival at a new shooting site to ensure the lighting is appropriate and backgrounds are clear of distractions. You need clear views of your subjects without branches or blades of grass in front of them and no distracting elements in the background.

Longer and faster lenses make it easier to blur out the background at wider apertures. Panning also blurs backgrounds when you're tracking birds in flight. Keep the focus area as close to the bird's head as possible and continue panning after the shutter closes. When you want to provide some context to your subject, try including some background, blurred out a little but still identifiable, to contrast with a tack-sharp subject.

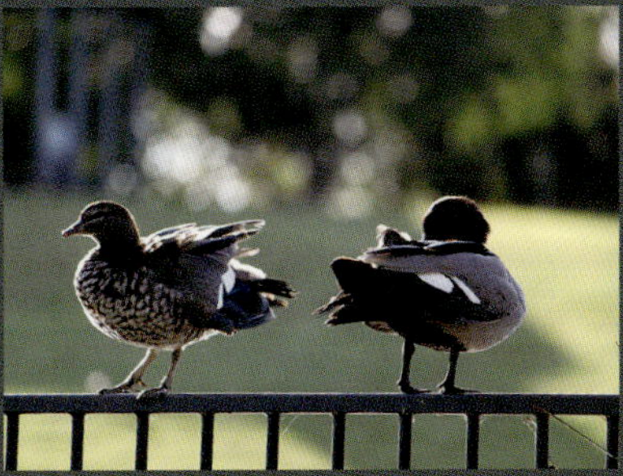

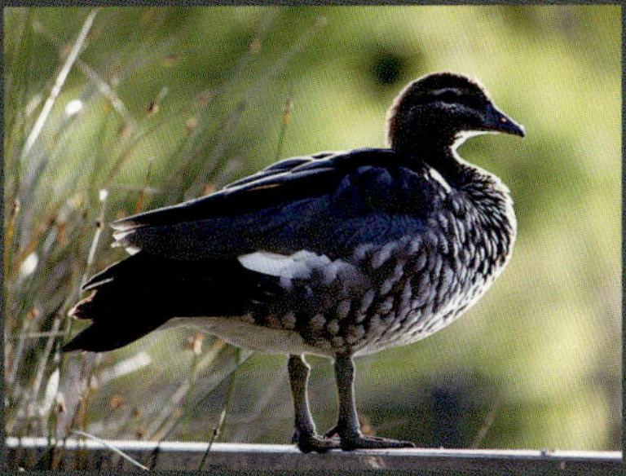

Even with a wide lens aperture the background in the upper image is distracting and has choppy bokeh. Zooming in to frame the shot on one of the birds provides a much more attractive picture. Canon EOS 500D with EF-S 55-250mm f/4-5.6 IS lens; ISO 100, 1/100 second at f/5.6; Aperture-priority AE with multi-pattern metering.

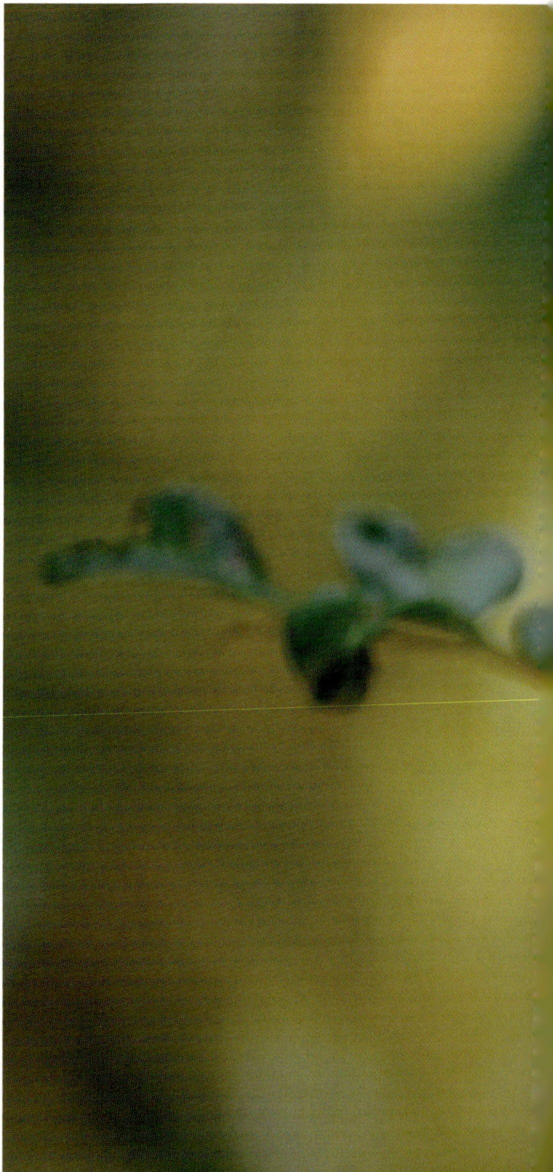

This shot of a Macleay's Honeyeater was taken at ISO 5000, a necessity as the photographer hand-held the camera and used a 600mm lens. Sony ILCE-9 camera with FE 200-600mm f/5.6-6.3 G OSS lens at 600mm, ISO 5000, Aperture-priority AE with centre-weighted metering; 1/320 second at f/6.3. Source: iStock by Camera House.

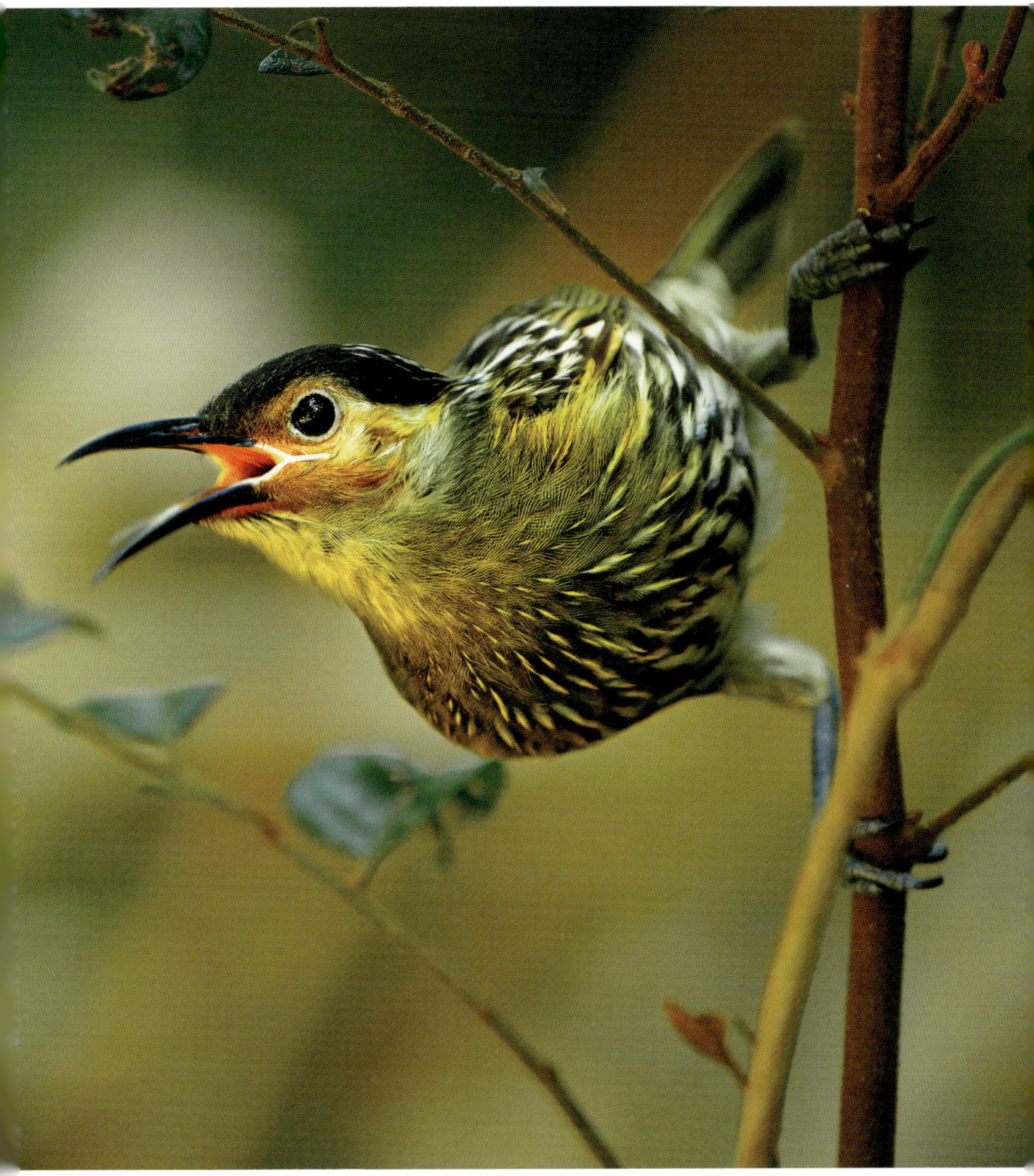

CHAPTER 7

USEFUL ACCESSORIES

Tripods

Some photographers like using a tripod whenever they photograph birds, while others find they are too much hassle to carry to the site and set up. There are valid reasons for either approach, which are outlined below.

Tripods are worth using whenever there's a risk of camera shake, particularly in the following situations:

1. When your camera isn't stabilised and you're using a long and heavy lens.
2. When you're shooting in dim lighting and you don't want to push the ISO speed too high. This is particularly true if you're shooting video.
3. When you're shooting with a remote control.

Make sure you allow enough time to set the tripod up correctly (see below). Follow these guidelines:

1. Adjust the height of the legs before you position the tripod and use the bubble level to ensure the camera isn't tilted. The centre post should be perpendicular to the ground when the legs are fully spread.
2. Since the central post is not as solid as the legs, don't rely on it for supporting the camera. Only use it for fine adjustments to ensure the camera is level.
3. Point one tripod leg towards the subject, keeping the others evenly-spaced behind when you're working on level ground. This improves stability and allows you to work from behind the camera. Reverse the process on a downhill slope, pointing two legs forwards for a more stable set-up.

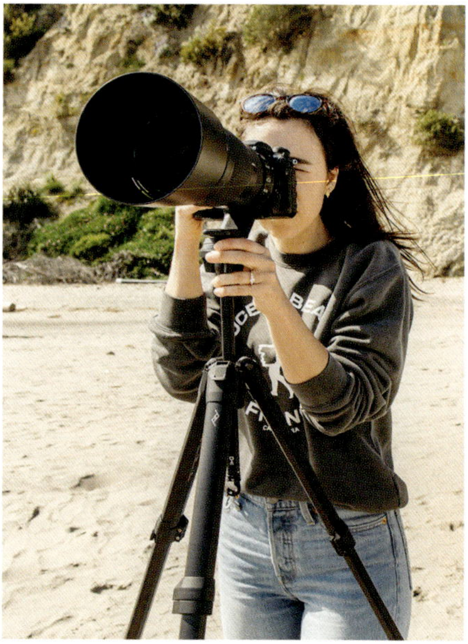

Tripod support is essential when you're using a long and heavy lens. (Source: Peak Design.)

4. When it's windy, hang a weighted bag on the centre column. A small bag containing rocks or cans of drink – or even your camera bag – will do.

5. If the lens has a tripod collar, attach the tripod to it to redistribute the weight and ensure your camera is well balanced on the support.

6. Match the feet on the tripod to the ground you're working on. Many tripods have screw-out spikes for use on slippery ground as well as rubber pads for smooth surfaces. Some tripods have interchangeable feet.

Gimbal heads, which are available for some tripods, give videographers a speedy way to recompose a shot or target an emerging subject quickly and smoothly. They also help to keep video footage smooth when the camera operator is tracking a moving bird.

They usually work best with longer and heavier lenses, providing controlled, damped movements and stability. Most gimbal heads accept Arca-compatible quick-release plates that can be attached to the lens's tripod foot or, with smaller lenses, to the camera.

Monopods

Monopods are a useful alternative to a tripod in some situations, although they don't provide as much stability since they only have one extendable leg to support the camera on a single point of contact with the ground. Many photographers find them less cumbersome than a tripod.

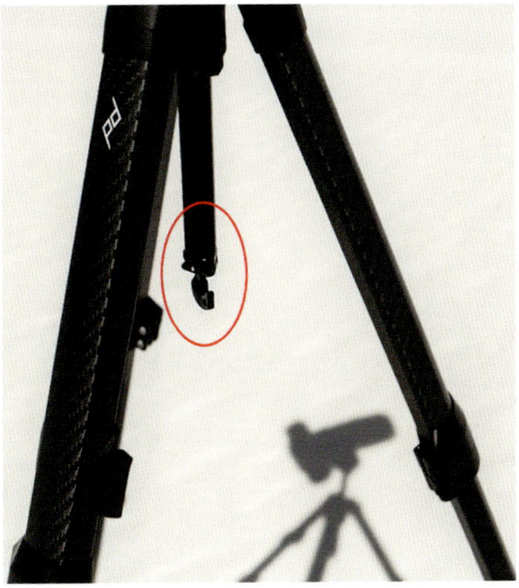

Better quality tripods have a hook at the bottom of their centre column (circled in red in this illustration) to allow you to hang a weight for added stability. (Source: Peak Design.)

They're also lighter and provide greater freedom to move around, which makes them a good choice when you want to travel light – including while flying in smaller aircraft when weight is heavily restricted. Setting up and adjusting a monopod is faster; you can attach the camera and extend the leg in just a few seconds. You can also tilt and swivel it in tight spaces where a tripod would be impractical.

However, monopods don't offer as much stability as tripods so they aren't suitable for situations that require rock-solid support, such as night shots. It can

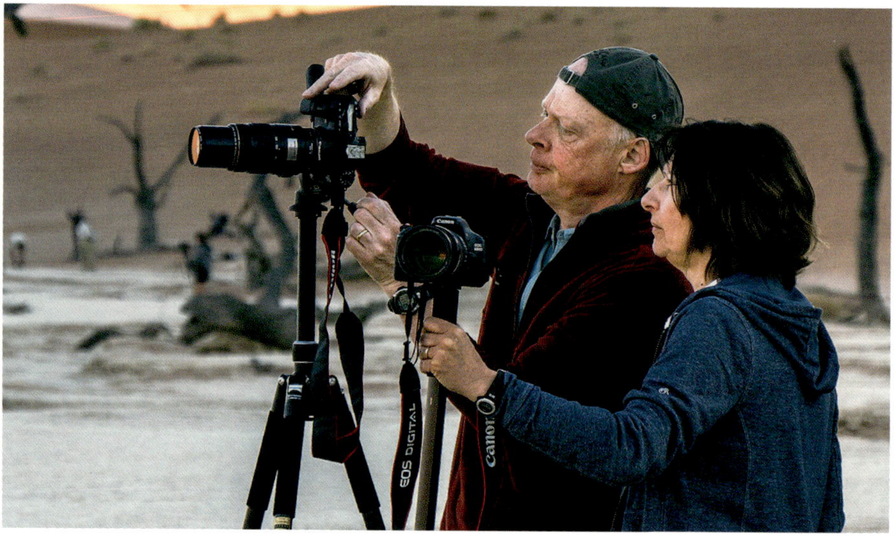

This illustration shows a tripod in use, along with a camera and lens on a monopod.

also be more difficult to keep a monopod upright and steady when there's a long and heavy lens on your camera.

Monopods are good when conditions require you to use shutter speeds a little slower than your hand-holdable limit. This can happen around sunrise and sunset, when many birds are active and pursuing behaviours not seen at other times of the day.

Teleconverters

Teleconverters normally consist of a magnifying lens (or lens assembly) that is inserted between the camera body and an existing lens to increase the focal length. A 2x teleconverter doubles the effective focal length, converting a 300mm lens to 600mm focal length. A 1.4x teleconverter increases the focal length of a 300mm lens to 420mm.

Buying a teleconverter certainly costs you less than buying a new lens with the increased focal length. It also means you have less weight to carry than if you had bought a longer lens.

Most teleconverters don't change the minimum focusing distance of the lens, a handy feature if you like taking close-ups. Some lens manufacturers produce lenses with built-in teleconverters that are perfectly matched to the main optics – although these lenses are usually relatively large and heavy.

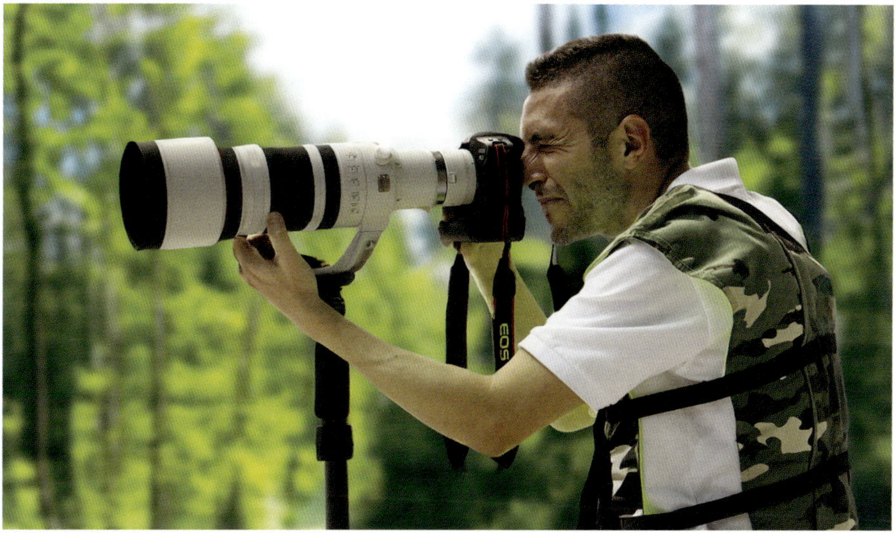

This illustration shows a monopod being used to support a super-telephoto lens, which has been attached to it via the tripod foot on the lens. (Source: Canon.)

Teleconverters have a few drawbacks, the main one being a loss of lens speed, which is proportional to the magnification factor. A 1.4x teleconverter reduces the maximum aperture of the lens by a full f-stop, while a 2x teleconverter cuts it by two full stops. So if you have a 300mm f/2.8 lens, adding a 1.4x converter gives you a 420mm f/4 lens, while adding a 2x teleconverter transforms it into a 600mm f/5.6 lens.

Reducing the light transmission can affect autofocusing since all AF systems depend on having enough light. On hot days, turbulence inside the lens barrel caused by air passing over dark surfaces is amplified by the magnification effect. Both can be serious issues for bird photographers.

Fitting a teleconverter also increases the effects of camera shake by the converter's magnification factor. This is true for both camera shake and subject motion. You'll need to increase the shutter speed and/or use a tripod/monopod to deal with this problem.

Adding more glass – and glass/air interfaces – to an existing lens can introduce optical aberrations and also magnify the effects of any aberrations in your original lens. Sharpness and contrast are the most likely to suffer and ghosting and flare can go from being minor irritants to serious problems.

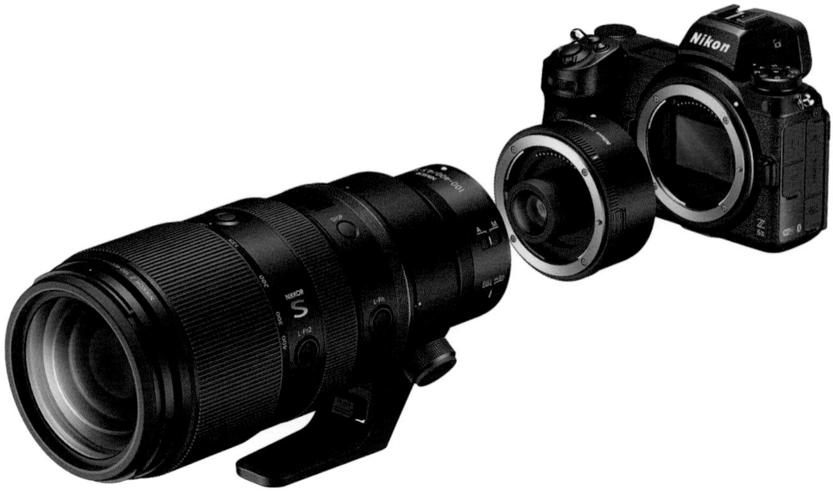

This illustration shows how a teleconverter fits in between the lens and the camera body, in this case effectively doubling the focal length of the lens, while at the same time halving its light-collecting capacity. (Source: Nikon.)

It's important to find a teleconverter that's fully compatible with your existing lens. Many teleconverters only work with one – or a small number of – lenses and some don't support autofocusing. Some don't cover the full range of the main lens and require manual focusing at close focusing distances or at specified aperture settings.

Filters

Modern digital cameras seldom benefit from the UV, skylight or haze filters that were popular for film cameras. Digital sensors are unaffected by UV radiation and there's always the risk of degrading the quality of the images you record by forcing the light to pass through inferior glass.

However, several types of filters can be worthwhile at times; notably Neutral density, graduated and polarising filters. Interestingly, these, too, are becoming obsolete since more and more cameras are being released with one or more of them built in.

Neutral density filters simply cut back the light entering the camera. They're used when you're shooting in bright conditions and can't access fast enough shutter speeds to let you open the lens aperture for isolating the subject from a distracting background.

They can also be helpful when the contrast between shadows and highlighted areas is too great for details to be recorded. However, this application has become less necessary with the arrival of cameras that can record HDR (high dynamic range) photos and videos.

Graduated filters are also losing popularity with cameras like the OM-1 Mark II introducing a Live Graduated ND function that lets users control how much of the frame is darkened by passing a fingertip across the screen, as shown in the illustrations on the next page.

Polarisers can be handy for suppressing reflections from water and are mainly used when taking location shots. They may also make small improvements to how feather textures are recorded. Circular polarisers are preferable to plane polarisers because you can rotate them to an angle to control the darkening gradient.

Other accessories

You need a suitable camera bag or backpack to carry your gear in when travelling to a shooting site. Other useful accessories include a pair of binoculars or a spotting scope to help you find the birds, and a guide app on your phone for identifying them.

Lens cleaning gear such as a blower brush and microfibre cloth will come in handy when on location and should be kept in your camera bag and checked at regular intervals. Your local camera shop can show you what's available and help you choose the most suitable items for your requirements.

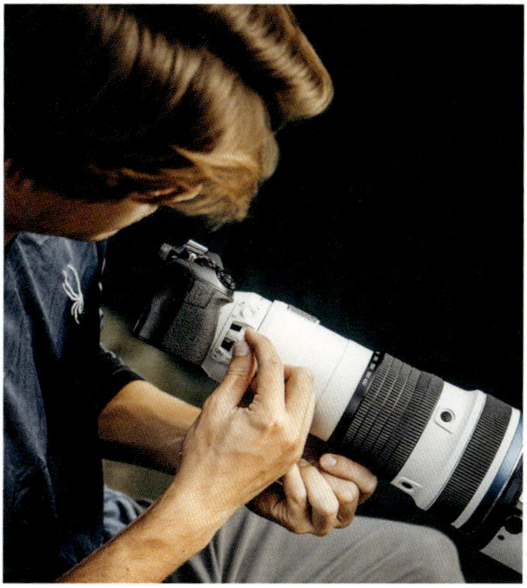

Lenses with built-in teleconverters make it easy to switch the magnification in and out, as shown in this illustration. (Source: OM Digital Solutions.)

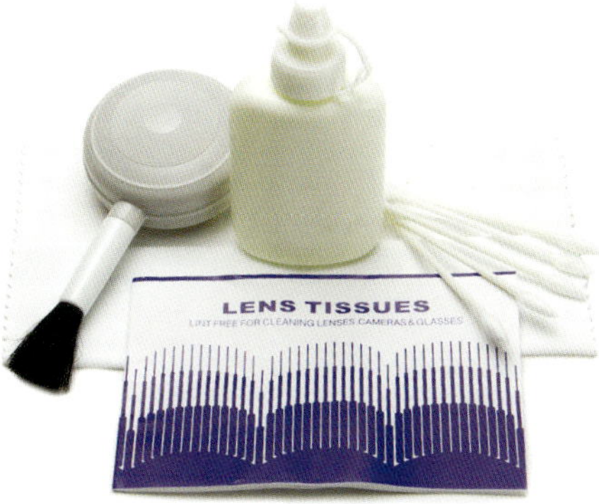

A lens cleaning kit won't take up much space in your camera bag but can help you keep your lenses grime-free, saving you time when you edit your images. (Source: Camera House.)

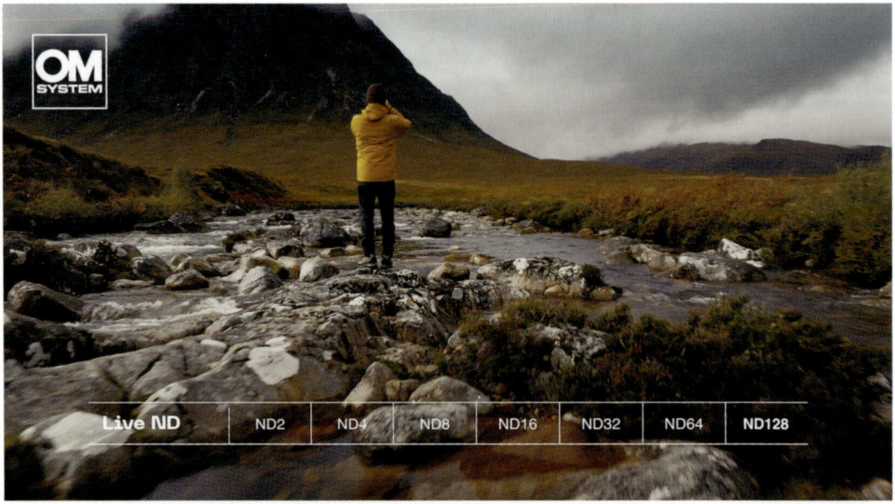

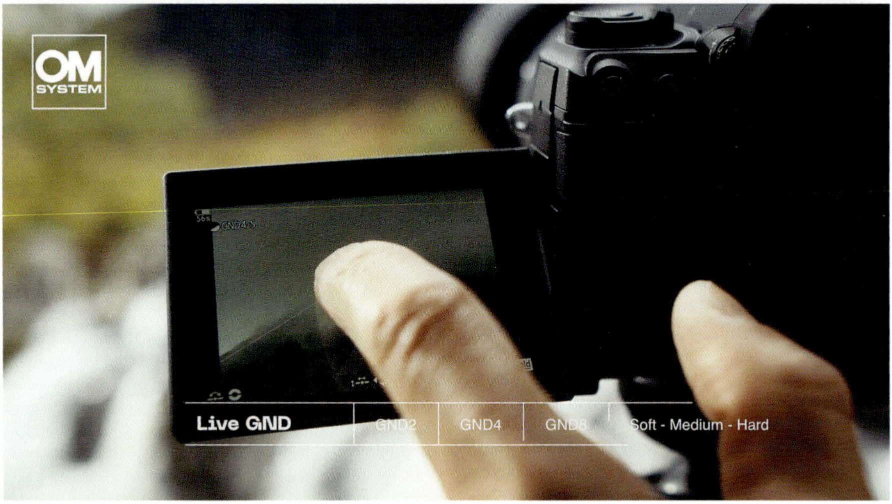

OM Systems was the first camera manufacturer to introduce both Live ND (top frame) and Live Graduated ND (lower frame) functions into its cameras. (Source: OM Digital Solutions.)

W See more *Photo Review* pocket guides at **www.photoreview.com.au/guides**